SONGS OF THE TETON SIOUX

Great West and Indian Series XXXIX

Songs of the Teton Sioux

by

HARRY W. PAIGE, Ph.D.

For the fires grow cold and the dances fail,
And the songs in their echoes die;
And what have we left but the graves beneath,
And, above, the waiting sky?
— THE SONG OF THE ANCIENT PEOPLE.

WESTERNLORE PRESS . . . 1970 . . . LOS ANGELES 90041

Library of Congress Catalog No. 78-110155

PRINTED IN THE UNITED STATES OF AMERICA BY WESTERNLORE PRESS

For My Father and Mother

Acknowledgments

IT IS my pleasure to acknowledge gratefully the assistance I received in the writing of this work. I am indebted to Dr. Shields McIlwaine, Professor Emeritus of English, State University of New York at Albany, for his patience, encouragement, hard work and imagination in the direction of the study which resulted in this book. I am also indebted to Dr. Perry D. Westbrook, Professor of English, State University of New York at Albany, for his critical reading of the manuscript and his helpful suggestions. To Mr. Stephen E. Feraca, Community Services Officer, Bureau of Indian Affairs, at the Seminole Agency in Hollywood, Florida, I owe a special debt of gratitude. His years of experience with the Tetons as a student and later as a member of the Bureau of Indian Affairs in the fields of Community Development and Adult Education at both the Pine Ridge and Rosebud Reservations eminently qualified him to make valuable suggestions in regard to Lakota language and Sioux life.

I am particularly grateful to Father Joseph Karol, S.J., of the St. Francis Mission in St. Francis, South Dakota for sharing his time and his great knowledge of the Lakota people with me. Also to my wife Ruth and to daughters, Judy and Sandy for joining me in my field work in South Dakota in 1964.

My thanks also go to the Research Foundation of State University of New York for its generous support of my field research in 1964 and 1965, and to the Division of Research, Clarkson College of Technology and the National Endowment for the Humanities for their support in 1968.

Finally, I should like to thank my informants, both Indian and white, whose co-operation and counsel made this study possible.

H. W. P.

1967

Clarkson College of Technology
Potsdam, New York

CONTENTS

ILLUSTRATIONS

Introduction

THIS WORK has been written in the belief that the rich body of literature in the oral tradition, created by the American Indians centuries before and after the arrival of the white man, is worthy of preservation and scholarly attention.

The purpose of this study is to investigate the origins and methods of Indian poetry as well as the human needs which inspired its development. The songs of the Teton or Western Sioux constitutes its primary subject matter. As with the language arts within the Western tradition, there are distinctions made between prose and poetry in primitive societies. Prose is the language of everyday affairs, while poetry is language clothed in dignity, seriousness, rhythm, form and cosmic belief by which the primitive sought understanding and ultimately power over the mysterious forces which surrounded him and shaped his environment. Poetry was his attempt to "trap the universal mystery in a net of magical words."

The present study attempts to present the characteristic features of the primitive imagination, the primitive's imaginative grasp of reality, which is so strikingly different from our own. The primitive, for example, does not recognize our dichotomies. In his life as in his art there are no Cartesian or Aristotelian cleavages to be reconciled. There is instead a sense of oneness which permeates his thought and is articulated in his poetry.

xiii

The poetry of the Sioux is analyzed for method and construction. Primitive poetry is highly impressionistic; therefore, symbolism is one of the keys to understanding, as it is in Indian graphic arts. The language of metaphor, secret language, archaic language, as well as the stylistic devices of contrast, variation, incremental repetition, parallelism, personification, apostrophe and euphony are examined in their relationship to the composition and purpose of the songs. Songs are classified according to types and placed in their traditional settings; e.g., individual and ceremonial, spiritual and secular, pure, and those showing evidence of cultural contact with outside influences. The probable degree of acculturation is considered by comparing older and more recent versions of ceremonial poetry. Problems of translation, such as the multiple meanings of words, the lack of abstract terms, and the difficulties of literal translation are investigated. The Lakota language itself is examined as an effective vehicle for the composition of primitive poetry. The study includes the recording, translation, interpretation and analysis of the songs of the Teton Sioux as a literary art form.

The study of Indian poetry is a study not only of the poems themselves, but the contexts in which they are presented. Many songs are absolutely meaningless without a knowledge of the setting in which they appear. The study of such poetry then must include examinations of relevant contexts — physical, psychological and spiritual.

Hence this work must also describe the Indians of the Plains — a people for whom the early nineteenth century was culturally a Golden Age. It was an epic age, an heroic age that existed in curious juxtaposition to the encroaching mechanical civilization. It was an age of hunting and warfare and the never-ending search for glory. It was a time in which an Odysseus or a Beowulf might have cried out for the moment to linger. Indeed, the struggles of Odysseus and his followers on their homeward journey seem reenacted in the odyssey of Chief Big Foot and his band of Sioux over the trail of tears, and Beowulf's struggle against *wyrd* seems as tragic as that of Sioux heroes, Crazy Horse and Red Cloud. Even the tragic inevitability of the Greek drama seems to hang over the Sioux Nation like an ominous cloud, threatening not only the individual hero, but the extinction of a people as well. No spot in Illium holds more tears than Wounded Knee.[1]

To the Sioux, singing was a natural function, his song representing usually either a spontaneous overflow of the emotions or a carefully disciplined contribution to a ceremony or ritual designed to bring about a specific end. In either case it seems as natural as breath. Primitive song was not art for art's sake, but for life's sake — an integral part of the primitive's being, for it was the one significant way in which he showed his dependency on the unseen powers. His songs covered human experience from birth to death, and even beyond to the "spirit trail."

To the modern reader the songs of the Sioux are a challenge. This challenge is to see through Indian eyes the world and man's relationship to it clearly, simply and with fresh vision and a new insight. Perhaps the challenge is not to see only, but to feel — to feel the magic and wonder and, at the same time, the reality of human experience which moved man to song.

H. W. P.

Rosebud, South Dakota, 1965.

[1]Wounded Knee, South Dakota is the site of the notorious Wounded Knee Massacre of December 29, 1890, in which approximately three hundred members of Chief Big Foot's band, mostly unarmed women and children, were slaughtered by members of the Seventh Cavalry.

CHAPTER ONE

The People

MODERN SCHOLARSHIP now contends that it is almost certain that the ancestors of the American Indian, robed in furs and carrying stone-tipped spears, came originally from Asia, across the Bering Strait and into North America, and thence to begin their migrations over two continents. According to the evidence of early archaeological discoveries, this probably happened over ten thousand years ago, during the period of the Pleistocene glaciations, and the people probably followed the protective valleys of the Wisconsin glacier which covered most of North America. Finally, these survivors of what must have been unimaginable hardships, stumbled upon a virgin land that, although not flowing with milk and honey, must have been full of the warmth of the sun and the coolness of water and the plenty of wild game. It may well be that at the journey's end a surge of victory, inarticulate yet full of a wild power, shook at least one breast to song.

From their northern point of entry into the new world these people must have been drawn in their incredible march by the sun's warmth and the relative security of the valleys, for they kept to a southerly course. Some of these bands settled in what is now the southern part of the United States, while others continued southward and into the present territories of Mexico and Central and South America, there to establish the civilizations that would become the great empires of the Inca and the Aztec.

The Sioux[1] were among the people who came originally from the southern part of the United States, referring to themselves at this time as the *Ocheti Sakowin*[2] or Seven Council Fires, and they were the most aggressive of all the Siouan tribes.

By the sixteenth century the Sioux had migrated to the headwaters of the Mississippi River, moving always northward, fighting as they went against the agricultural societies with whom they came in contact and against whom they had the usual intense prejudice of an agricultural-hunting society for a farming community. When first seen by the whites, then, in the seventeenth century, the Sioux were a forest people. Early in the same century the Sioux fought a long series of wars with the Algonquins who, because they had obtained firearms from the French and English, were able to drive the Sioux into what is now southern Minnesota. During these early migrations, of which no extensive account is available, the Sioux divided into the Eastern, Middle and Western groups. The Eastern Sioux settled permanently in the wooded country west of Lake Superior while the Tetons or Western division became the Plains Sioux and were destined to settle across the Missouri River. Warfare, migrations and tribal feuds did much to promote further divisions of the Sioux so that the cultures of the Eastern, Middle and Western divisions of the Sioux became more disparate.

About the year 1760 the Teton Sioux invaded the territory of the Great Bend of the Missouri River and found themselves thwarted in their westward march by the Arikara, who were mounted and armed by the Spanish.[3] Lewis and Clark reported that in 1804 the Arikara were successful in preventing the Sioux from crossing the Missouri[4] until sometime be-

[1]*Sioux* is a French corruption of an Algonquin word for *snake*, and thus, by metaphor, *enemy*. The Tetons referred to themselves as *Lakota*, which means *allies*.

[2]George E. Hyde, *Red Cloud's Folk* (Norman, Oklahoma, 1957), p. 3.

[3]Hyde, *Red Cloud's Folk*, p. 17.

[4]Meriwether Lewis and William Clark, *The Journals of Lewis and Clark* (New York, 1964), p. 58.

tween 1772 and 1780 the Arikaras were all but wiped out by three widespread epidemics of smallpox.[5]

During their contact with the Arikaras or Rees the Sioux probably obtained a few horses through trade or plunder, but could not be called a nation of horsemen until the last decade of the eighteenth century. In about 1775 the war parties of the Sioux, led in their westward march by the Oglala[6] division of the tribe, crossed the Missouri and, in 1775 or 1776, Standing Bull, an Oglala war chief, discovered *Paha Sapa* or the Black Hills, later regarded as the sacred lands of the Sioux.[7] The Brules soon followed their kinsmen across the Missouri and into the territory of the powerful and then hostile Cheyennes, who claimed the Black Hills region as their own.

Although the Tetons at this time still considered the eastern woodlands as their home,[8] their semi-annual hunting expeditions across the Missouri introduced them to a land full of buffalo herds, abundant grass and water supplies, natural protection and all the elements that were attractive to a semi-nomadic, adventurous people. Just as the thought and way of life of the ancient Greeks was influenced by the geography of mountains and sea, so the Tetons were shaped by the wild exhilaration of the vast, sweeping plains and the limitless expanse of horizon. They came to love the freedom of almost pure democracy and the mystical religion of visions and dreams induced by the solitude, the painfully blue sky, the bright sun and the wealth of *WakaNtaNka's* plenty. During these excursions across the Missouri, the Tetons acquired more horses, and later drove the Cheyennes (*Shahiyela* or People of Alien Speech) from the Black Hills.

[5]Hyde, *Red Cloud's Folk,* p. 20.

[6]The Oglala are one of the divisions of the Teton Sioux. In Lakota, *oglala* is a verb meaning "he scatters his own." Later, the Oglala were known as Red Cloud's people and the Pine Ridge Sioux.

[7]Hyde, *Red Cloud's Folk,* p. 20.

[8]*Ibid.,* p. 21.

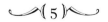

The crossing of the Missouri and the acquisition of more horses were events of the greatest significance in the early history of the Sioux. Their kinsmen east of the Missouri traveled on foot, with only dogs to pull the *travois* which carried their possessions for hunting, warfare and homemaking. After the Tetons became mounted, however, about the year 1796, a revolution was wrought in their way of life. Their mobility, and therefore their striking power, were greatly increased. They could chase down and kill the *pte* or buffalo, building their economy on the hunting of this shaggy beast that roamed the prairie in herds of thousands. They could take the initiative and attack their new enemies of the plains — the Crow, the Pawnee and the Shoshone. They could develop their young men into expert horse warriors so that less than a century later one of the most respected of Indian fighters, General George Crook, would pay tribute to them as "the finest light cavalry in the world."

There are many descriptions of the Sioux and their way of life from those who lived among them or traded with them, or attempted with varying degrees of success to convert them to the Christian faith.[9] There are the reports of the "squaw men" who married Sioux women and were often accepted into the Indian society as brothers. Most accounts agree that they were a superior people physically, mentally and morally. Many of the men were over six feet tall, with strong disciplined bodies and classical features. The women, who were well treated by the Sioux, were tall, graceful and slender, presenting a marked contrast to the women of the desert tribes, who were short and heavy set.

The period from the acquisition of horses to about 1860 was the Golden Age of the Teton Sioux, as their Winter Counts[10] testify. During this time they were the lords of the plains, each warrior a paladin who found no dearth of oppor-

[9]See Bibliography for works which offer these descriptions.

[10]Winter Counts were pictographs on buffalo hides depicting the event for which the year was remembered, e.g., 1876 is known on one such Winter Count as *Pehin HaNska ktepi* or Winter in which they killed Custer.

tunity to count *coup*[11] on his enemies and steal their horses and women. It was not only the Sioux economy that depended on the buffalo hunt and warfare, but the social systems as well. Unless he distinguished himself in hunting or warfare the Sioux walked an alien path. Glory, honor and wealth were all to be won on the warpath. The rewards of tribal society and sacred institutions were contingent upon a warrior's success in battle and on the hunt. The rights of manhood, courtship and marriage all depended on this system of courage and honor in war, as the song of this Indian maiden testifies:

howe	You may
zuya ya ye	go on the warpath.
tokśa	When
caze	your name
nacihon	I hear (announced among the victors)
kinhan	then
hingna ciyin kte.[12]	I will marry you.

Even a young man's name could be considered a gain of war, as formal name-taking ceremonies usually took place after the young warrior had earned distinction on the field of battle. It was a society that allowed few alternatives, among them glory or death.

Warfare was not only a means of acquiring horses — it was a glorious adventure, a game to the Plains Indians, and the Sioux were its champions.[13] Theirs was a quixotic approach to warfare, for its ultimate end was not so much victory as it was individual distinction. In many ways warfare

---

[11]*Coup* is the French word for *blow* and referred to the act of striking an enemy with a wand-like stick, a bow or sometimes with the hand. This was held to be the greatest distinction which a warrior could win in battle.

[12]Frances Densmore, *Teton Sioux Music* (Washington, 1918), pp. 370-371. This text contains the following errors: *caze* in 1.4 should be *caje* and *nacihon* in 1.5 should be *nawahon*. The reader is referred to Appendix II for a Pronunciation Key.

[13]Robert H. Lowie, *Indians of the Plains* (Garden City, New York, 1963), p. 114.

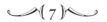

on the plains resembled that of the feudal system in the middle ages and the spirit resembled the *comitatus* spirit of the Anglo-Saxon period. Many times a warrior returning from an engagement in which many of the enemy had been killed and many horses stolen reported that "nothing had happened," which simply meant that he had counted no *coup*, taken no scalp, rescued no fallen comrade. It may have been a magnificent victory for the war party, but if the individual warrior had nothing to sing of, then it was at best a hollow victory for him. During these years the Sioux had few guns and long range encounters were not their idea of warfare. They called the white man's version of war "just shooting" as it permitted no truly heroic deeds as the Sioux counted them.

Even during the Golden Age of the Sioux, however, there was a handwriting on the wall for those "far-seeing" ones among them. The nineteenth century brought with it a host of French traders from St. Louis, who began large scale trading operations among the Tetons. During this period of cultural proximity, the influence of traders representing rival companies could be used as an index to the actions of large groups of the Sioux. They moved their hunting grounds, attacked neighboring tribes and fought the whites according to the particular influence they were under at the time. Most of the Tetons had by this time developed a fondness for the white man's articles of trade and many considered them a necessity, especially guns and ammunition, cloth, metal utensils and objects of adornment. The French, using all their business acumen and years of experience with the Indians, attempted to get the chiefs to trade exclusively with their company and thereby gain a monopoly on this lucrative industry. Sometimes, as a business expedient, these traders married Sioux women and so increased their influence among the Indian people. But the Frenchman's greatest trade item was bad liquor.

The introduction of *mniwakaN* or "mysterious water" to the Plains Indians marked the beginning of a gradual deterioration of the moral code under which they lived. Liquor demoralized the wild Indian: its effects robbed him not only of his senses but of pride and self-respect and served to weaken his resistance to the many diseases of the whites. Tribal killings, extremely rare among the Sioux who considered killing a brother Sioux the worst of all crimes, became all too frequent. Sioux women were sold to the whites for liquor. The chiefs, unable to control their young warriors and their thirst for liquor, lost their tribal authority. The notorious *Wagluhe* or Followers, a sizable faction of Indians weak in will and spirit who preferred the soft ways and whiskey of the WaśicuN (whites), increased in number and influence. Detribalized, these Indians touched both societies yet belonged to neither. The father of Red Cloud, tragic Oglala chieftain, died a drunkard's death. Many others followed the *WaśicuN* road to degradation and despair until the mystical "sacred hoop," which bound the Sioux Nation in spiritual unity under *WakaNtaNka*, threatened to break. It was only then, from the darkness of despair, that giants arose from Mother Earth, spilling whiskey rather than a brother's blood.

In 1822 a comet, recorded by white men of science, blazed in the western sky, describing an arc of fire over an Oglala village where a woman had just given birth to a son. The wise men of the tribe considered this a powerful omen, a sign from *WakaNtaNka*, this fire-in-the-sky, and so the infant was appropriately named *Mahpiya Luta*. The whites were to translate his name as Red Cloud, a name destined to assume a major role in the history of the Sioux. As if in answer to a people's supplications other leaders arose: Crazy Horse, Sitting Bull, Spotted Tail, Two Strike, and Gall. The list reads like a roll call of Sioux culture heroes.

Even giants were not enough to save the Sioux, however. They could only win a brief reprieve against the inevitable fate of the primitive in conflict with the forces of "progress" and the interests of those people who had glimpsed their manifest destiny, symbolized by the enormous potential of the virgin lands beyond the Missouri. Between this emerging nation and its vision stood the implacable Red Man, the Stone Age savage defying the industrial might of a growing society. Progress, like nature, it would seem, abhors a vacuum, or what is considered as such by its advocates.

The final period of Sioux history, from the 1860s to 1891, then, is the tragic record of a people's death song, interrupted by moments of triumph made more bitter by their brevity. The destruction of the Sioux was one of a tragic, relentless gradualism. As the Greek gods played with Oedipus, permitting him his illusory victories over Fate, so the unseen powers played with the Sioux, permitting them their glory on the Rosebud and at the Little Big Horn before the final tragedy at Wounded Knee. But even as the Sioux celebrated their triumphs by victory dances, kill talks and songs there were those among them who looked ahead and saw the ashen spectre of ultimate defeat, and their hearts became heavy with the burden they knew they must carry, not only for themselves, but for their people as well. Sick at heart, Red Cloud, once the very spirit of Sioux resistance, who had forced the closing of the Bozeman Trail and the abandonment of Fort Phil Kearny, capitulated to the inevitable and made peace with the whites who promised in the Treaty of 1868 that the Sioux should hold their sacred lands and hunting grounds. Spotted Tail, famous Brule rival of Red Cloud, also saw that the future of the Sioux, if indeed they had a future, lay in their willingness to follow the "black road" of the white man. Later, Red Cloud and Spotted Tail, as well as other agency Indians, were regarded as traitors by the non-progressives who were still "out" and who followed Crazy Horse to the Powder River country, home of most of the hostiles. Both Sitting Bull and Crazy Horse, irreconciliable to the ways of the whites, preferred freedom and possible death as an alternative to captivity and imitation of the whites.

There were those among the whites who protested vehemently against what they considered to be a shameful treatment of the Indian. Most of these well-intentioned people were Eastern "do-gooders" who were as unrealistic in their aspirations for the Indian as their opponents were barbaric. Many of these whites, inspired by Christian idealism, actually believed that they could drag the Indian from the Stone Age into modernity in a few short years, although it had never been done before in the history of the world. The leash which was to be used to lead them was to be agriculture.

From their earliest days on the plains the Sioux had been the bitter foe of all farming societies. The Sioux were warriors and hunters by long tradition and looked with contempt on those who would "scratch the earth" for food. The Sioux would not even permit their women to engage in such a lowly pursuit. Another reason for their deep-rooted antipathy for agriculture was a religious one: they considered *WakaNtaNka* as their spiritual Father and Mother Earth as their Mother. They believed that farming was an outrage against Mother Earth, that to scar her bosom with hoe or plow was to violate her and so bring bad times to their people by making them out of touch with the higher powers. There were other considerations that the "friends" of the Sioux overlooked in their desire to promote agriculture and force the Indian to imitate the alien ways of the whites. Even if the Sioux could have been converted to agriculture, the land could not. Poor, flinty soil, prolonged periods of drought, grasshoppers and locusts — all conspired against this grand design. Had these "friends" of the Sioux had knowledge and understanding as well as sympathy, they might have had a far greater effect on Indian policy, perhaps to the benefit of all concerned.

Another obstacle to progress in Indian affairs was the constant feuding between the War Department and the Indian Bureau, which moved under the jurisdiction of the Department of the Interior in 1849. The military was anxious to maintain a strict and consistent policy of control, while the "friends" and the Indian Bureau wanted to accomplish the same ends by gradual methods. The split was disastrous. Peaceful Indians were destroyed by the military, who often could not tell a friendly band from hostiles, and the strong among the reservation Indians intimidated the weak, often corrupt agents of the Indian Bureau. From the President of the United States down to the lowest Indian Bureau clerk there was no consistent policy in dealing with the Indians. In addition to the existing confusion, there was a change of administration every four years and often a radical change in policy which accompanied the process. To the Sioux this inconsistency was to be interpreted as weakness on the part of the whites. Dishonest agents, who sometimes retired for life after a few short years of diverting Indian funds and goods into their own pockets, and sadistic military leaders who murdered women and children in "battle," confirmed the Indian conviction that the whites were never to be trusted. The Northern Cheyenne, long time allies of the Sioux, in eloquent testimony to the duplicity of the whites, called them *veho*, which means *spider* in their tongue.[14]

The Sioux and the Cheyenne were more than allies: they were kinsmen. Because they struggled against a common enemy, and because they shared a common plains culture, their individual lives and their fate as a people were intertwined. The two peoples intermarried, camped together and shared most of the same ceremonials, including the Sun Dance. At one time the camp of Oglala Chief Crazy Horse contained more Cheyenne warriors than Sioux. The early massacres of the Cheyennes, therefore, had vast repercussions among all Indians of the Plains, especially the Sioux. These early tragedies served to crystallize the attitudes of the two peoples: no more could the whites be trusted; no more were the Plains Indians, even those designated as "friendly," safe from the ruthless policy of extermination that threatened all. It was better to die fighting, they concluded. The massacre of the peaceful Cheyennes at Sand Creek was

[14]Mari Sandoz, *Cheyenne Autumn* (New York, 1953), p. 20.

a terrible and dramatic refutation of the appeasement poli-
cies of the influential "progressive" Indians who believed
that the whites would honor their treaties and the words of
the Grandfather in Washington. "Remember Sand Creek!"
became the battle cry of Sioux and Cheyenne alike. It may
be no exaggeration to say that nearly all of the engagements
that followed the Sand Creek Massacre stemmed from it. It
was the torch that fired the prairie.

Colonel Chivington's unprovoked attack on the village of
Black Kettle and White Antelope toward the end of the
Moon of the Falling Leaves (November 29, 1864) plunged
the frontier into the bloodiest series of conflicts of the Indian Wars in America. This infamous slaughter of a peaceful
Cheyenne village whose chiefs had been given a pledge of
peace by the governor of Colorado and the military at Fort
Lyon only thirty miles from Sand Creek, was termed by a
Congressional Investigation Committee as "perhaps the
foulest and most unjustifiable crime in the annals of America." Only weeks before the tragedy, Black Kettle and White
Antelope had turned in more than half of their weapons as
a gesture of good faith. The massacre, led by an ex-Meth-
odist preacher, fanatic in his un-Christian determination to
exterminate the Indian, actively encouraged his troops to
destroy the handful of warriors present, murder and scalp
women and children and smash the infants against trees.
White Antelope stood bravely before Chivington's Second
Colorado Cavalry singing his death song: "Nothing lives
long, except the earth and the mountains." Then he was cut
down by a hail of bullets, almost under the shadow of the
American flag raised by the Cheyennes in the futile hope
that it would afford the village immunity from the "wagon
guns" (cannon) of the soldiers. When the slaughter was
finally over, over three hundred Cheyenne lay dead on the
freezing ground, two hundred of them women and children.

Exactly ten years before the massacre at Sand Creek the
first blood of the white soldiers had been shed after the hot-
headed Lieutenant Grattan had ordered Brule Chief Con-

quering Bear shot down after a dispute over the killing of a cow worth ten dollars. After the Chief fell, Grattan and all thirty-two of his men were hacked to pieces by the enraged Brules. If the Grattan affair marked the beginning of the Sioux Wars, then the Sand Creek Massacre was the culmination of white treachery. From that time on the memory of the massacre was carved into the hearts of the Indians of the plains. Chivington himself wrote the footnote to perfidy when he closed his official report: "All did nobly."[15]

The few survivors of the massacre "carried the pipe" to their kinsmen, the Northern Cheyenne, and then to the Sioux war chiefs Sitting Bull of the Hunkpapas and Crazy Horse of the Oglalas. Heartsick and furious, the Sioux chiefs smoked the pipe with their brothers, and soon the Plains Indians were organized as never before.[16] In the months that followed, thousands of whites, most of them completely innocent, fell beneath the wrath of the Indians, while Chivington, who had perpetrated the massacre, returned home in triumph, exhibiting Indian scalps and severed limbs to a cheering crowd in a Denver theatre.

By this time the War Department had won its long struggle with the Indian Bureau, and their "get tough" policy had gained much popular support, especially in the west. Public reaction against the Indian was at a new high. The Homestead Act of 1862 had sent people pouring across the Missouri and into Indian Territory. The Civil War ended in 1865, and troops used to free the black man could now be spared to help exterminate the Indian.

In the winter of 1868, on the banks of the Washita in Indian Territory (Oklahoma), lay the village of Black Kettle, who had survived the massacre at Sand Creek and who had fought vigorously for peace since that dark November day.

[15]J. M. Chivington, quoted in George Bird Grinnell, *The Fighting Cheyennes* (Norman, Oklahoma, 1958), p. 174.

[16]George Bird Grinnell, *The Fighting Cheyennes* (Norman, Oklahoma, 1958), p. 181.

At dawn on November twenty-seventh a bugle sounded and the Seventh Cavalry fell on Black Kettle's people, killing over one hundred, again mostly women and children. This time Chief Black Kettle did not escape; he and his wife fell before the opening of their lodge in a crazy pattern of violent death. The leader of the soldiers that day was the popular boy-general of the Civil War — Lieutenant Colonel George Armstrong Custer, who hoped to put an end to the Indian Wars. The Cheyenne and the Sioux marked the name well, and vowed to avenge the blood of their fallen friends and relatives.

Seven years later, in 1875, Custer and his Seventh Cavalry "scouted" the Black Hills on a military "surveying" expedition, and came out of the hills triumphantly announcing that he had found gold. Soon the Black Hills region, won by the Sioux in battle and granted by the Treaty of 1868, was alive with gold-seeking whites. For the Sioux and the Cheyenne it was an open declaration of war, a fight to the end.

In June of the next year General George Crook, with one thousand soldiers, attacked the camp of Crazy Horse on Rosebud Creek and was badly defeated by the Oglala war chief. Crazy Horse's defeat of Crook on the Rosebud prepared the way for the greatest of all Indian victories — the total annihilation of Custer and his Seventh Cavalry at the Little Big Horn on June 25, 1876, with Crazy Horse and Gall generally considered to be the Indian military leaders behind the triumph.

The victory over Custer was in one sense the beginning of the end for the Sioux. The entire American nation, in the midst of celebrating its centennial, was humiliated as never before by the Custer defeat. The campaign against the Sioux was stepped up. General Miles demanded that one half of the United States' forces be sent to Sioux territory to crush what was represented as a savage horde. Reprisals soon followed. Old American Horse was attacked and killed at the Battle of Slim Buttes. Sitting Bull fled to Canada, and Crazy Horse was killed by a soldier at Fort Robinson in

September of 1877. Without their two greatest leaders, the remaining hostiles were split into small bands, hunted down and placed on reservations.

There for the next dozen years the Sioux endured a living death of despair, starvation and beggary in the concentration camp atmosphere of the reservations, while the whites followed what the Sioux called the "Thieves' Road" across their lands to the Black Hills. On the reservations the Sioux starved, sickened and waited for death; their only escapes, liquor and the fading glories of a remembered past. Despite the guarantee of the American constitution the Sioux were forced to abandon their ancient, traditional rituals including the annual Sun Dance and even the *Heyoka* ceremony, the clown dance, performed by those who had dreamed of the Thunderbeings. He was discouraged from speaking his own language. Great pressures were exerted to Christianize the Sioux by un-Christian methods. The Indians saw through the paradox, and kept the old ways alive in their hearts. Then, with dramatic suddenness in the winter of 1889, the Sioux responded to a last, desperate attempt to survive as Indians, the call of the Indian Messiah who introduced the craze that would be known as the Ghost Dance.

Wovoka, who began it all, was a full-blooded Paiute Indian who had lived with the whites in his youth and was known to them as Jack Wilson. His father, Tavibo, was a Paiute shaman and dreamer who had spoken often of a day of paradise regained by the Indian, but with his death and his son's departure to live with a white family named Wilson, the message seemed to die on the winds. But it was from the Wilsons and their talk of Jehovah and Christ that Wovoka was to build his hybrid doctrine, half-Christian and half-native. Wovoka then left the whites forever and returned to his people with his "new" religion.

That same year Wovoka was stricken with scarlet fever and after a long siege, finally felt himself recovering as the old year died. He had apparently discovered in the white man's almanac that there was to be an eclipse of the sun in

January of 1889.[17] When Wovoka recovered from his illness, as the eclipse ended, he told his people that he had entered the spirit world and had talked with God, and that God had told him of the end of the world — for the whites. For God had presented Himself to the whites and they had rejected Him and had crucified Him. Now God would come again, this time to His Indian brothers, who would receive Him well. The earth was to be covered by a great flood, and from the deluge it would be reborn. The elk, the deer, and especially the buffalo would reappear, and all the things of nature that had made the "long ago" times good. All the Indians would be young again, and all Indian tribes would be bound together, united under God. The whites were to be swallowed up by the earth. All the Indian had to do was to wait and have faith — and dance.

As the whites celebrated the admission of the Dakotas into the Union (November 2, 1889) the Sioux were once again alive as a people and waiting for more news of the *Wanekia* or "makes lives savior." They decided to send a delegation led by Kicking Bear of the Cheyenne River Agency and Short Bull of the Rosebud Agency to Walker Lake, Nevada to meet the new Messiah. They went, and they believed as others had done that the Second Coming had arrived, and the Indian had become God's chosen people. The ghost religion spread like a prairie fire, fanned by the dry winds of despair, and before long a great many tribes were under its spell.

The Ghost Dance was undoubtedly partly Christian and partly a regeneration of older Indian beliefs. The Indians were taught by its high priests to sing ghost songs and dance a slow, shuffling drag step in a circle, men and women dancing together ceremonially for the first time. The dance was to be non-violent, the Messiah pleading with the delegates to "do always right." They were to dance until they fell into

[17] Wovoka had "some little knowledge of English" according to James Mooney in *The Ghost Dance Religion and the Sioux Outbreak of 1890* (Chicago, 1965), p. 13.

a trance or "died" and came back to life with stories of having seen their dead again. As they danced they chanted hypnotically:

> The Father says so — E'yayo!
> The Father says so — E'yayo!
> The Father says so,
> The Father says so.
> You shall see your Grandfather — E'yayo!
> You shall see your Grandfather — E'yayo!
> The Father says so,
> The Father says so.
> You shall see your kindred — E'yayo!
> You shall see your kindred — E'yayo!
> The Father says so,
> The Father says so.[18]

The new religion had all the usual characteristics of Indian devotion — mysticism, escapism and elaborate ritual. It also had a quality of pathetic desperation common to all primitive religions whose advocates feel they are becoming extinct in an alien, hostile environment.

The Ghost Dance Religion as handed down by its prophet, Wovoka, was, of course, modified and revised as it was carried back to the tribes by the delegates. The Sioux added one significant feature, an article of clothing, the bullet-proof "ghost shirt," the wearing of which was to render the believer immune to the bullets of the whites. This provision anticipated violence, and therefore altered Wovoka's original doctrine of peace and patience. Other purification and fasting rites taken from older ceremonies were innovations of the Tetons, adding to the scope and dimension of the complex.

It was not long before the whites became alarmed. There were dark rumors that the agency Sioux were on the verge of going out to join the hostiles, who were the most militant disciples of the Ghost Dance. Old and almost blind, Chief Red Cloud, settled at the Pine Ridge Agency and a nominal

---

[18] Mooney, *The Ghost Dance Religion*, p. 297.

convert to Roman Catholicism, expressed the sentiment that he would not interfere with the new religion of the people.[19] Sitting Bull, returned from his sojourn in Canada to the Standing Rock Agency, was far too practical a man to believe in the new religion, but he, like Red Cloud, would not discourage his people's belief in the Ghost Dance, for had the Grandfather in Washington (President Harrison) not boasted that all of his children had the freedom to worship, each one at his own altar? Despite his skepticism, Sitting Bull was regarded by many as the leader of the Ghost Dance movement, and Agent McLaughlin conspired to have the old chief arrested by the Indian police. In a bloody preface to the final chapter of the Sioux, Sitting Bull was killed while "resisting arrest" on December 15, 1890.

When the news of Sitting Bull's death spread across the plains and the reservations the Sioux were frantic with grief and fear. Old and wise chiefs had to labor day and night attempting to calm their young warriors and prevent them from joining the hostiles and the Ghost Dancers in the strongholds of the Bad Lands. One of the bands still "out" was that of *SitaNka* or Big Foot and his Minneconjous. When orders were issued for his arrest, he and his ragged, starving band of two hundred and fifty women and children and less than one hundred warriors slipped away from the soldiers guarding them on the night of December 22.

At first, Big Foot planned to go to the stronghold in the Bad Lands and join the Ghost Dancers,[20] but the illness that had plagued him in recent weeks had developed into pneumonia. He decided that he would lead his people to the Pine Ridge Agency and appeal to Red Cloud for help for him and his people.

When it was discovered that Big Foot and his band had escaped the Army, two thousand soldiers were sent into the field in hot pursuit. Major Whiteside, leading a battalion of

[19]George E. Hyde, *A Sioux Chronicle* (Norman, Oklahoma, 1956), p. 254.

[20]Hyde, *A Sioux Chronicle*, p. 297.

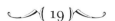

CHAPEL AT SITE OF THE WOUNDED KNEE MASSACRE

Custer's old Seventh Cavalry, intercepted the band and escorted them to a camping area near a creek that the Sioux called *CaNkpe Opi* — Wounded Knee — only seventeen miles from the relative safety of the agency at Pine Ridge.[21] When the Major demanded that Big Foot surrender, the old chief complied at once. Big Foot was now desperately ill and delirious with fever and his people were half-frozen and starving. He explained to the bearded Major that he would have surrendered before had he known where to find the soldiers.

Whiteside ordered the Indians to camp in a valley, directly beneath the hill where he had placed his Hotchkiss guns. The next morning, December 29, Colonel Forsyth relieved the Major, and one of his first orders was to disarm the prisoners. The troopers of the Seventh, mostly raw recruits with little discipline and the blot of Custer's defeat on their unit, began the search for weapons. They showed little respect for property or the privacy of the women in their angry search.[22]

Big Foot's medicine man, Yellow Bird, began shouting that the Ghost Shirts would protect the believers from the bullets of the "bluecoats," and as he threw a handful of magic dust into the air, a shot rang out.[23]

What followed can only be described as a butchering of the innocents. Big Foot, propped up on a makeshift stretcher, was cut down by the bullets. Almost all of his warriors were killed or struck down in the first volley fired by the troops. Most of the soldiers who fell were caught in the deadly cross fire of their own comrades. Women and children were pursued and struck down as far as three miles from the scene of the "battle" by the enraged soldiers of the Seventh. The cry, "Remember Custer!" was heard to resound in the cold air in the intervals between the deadly chatter of the Hotchkiss guns.

[21]Hyde, *A Sioux Chronicle*, p. 298.
[22]Mooney, p. 115.
[23]*Ibid.*, p. 118.

When it was over, thirty-five soldiers and an Indian scout lay dead or dying. The Indian losses will never be known, for that evening a Dakota blizzard set in and the soldiers, bearing their wounded and a few prisoners, retreated to the agency at Pine Ridge.

It was three days before they returned to the field at Wounded Knee. Some of the Indian dead had been stolen away by relatives and friends for secret burial. Others, wounded and nearly frozen to death, still lay next to the dead bodies on the ground. Estimates of the Indian dead numbered about three hundred. A detail of white civilians was paid by the number of bodies to bury the Indian dead, while a detachment of soldiers stood by in case the enraged Indians should appear seeking revenge. The detail dug a trench fifty feet long and six feet wide and then, without the benefit of Christian or native rites, dumped the frozen bodies into the common grave.

Years later, in his autobiography, Black Elk, an Oglala holy man, who had been at the Little Big Horn and had witnessed the aftermath at Wounded Knee, summarized the impact of the tragedy:

I did not know then how much was ended. When I look back now from this high hill of my old age, I can see the butchered women and children lying heaped and scattered all along the crooked gulch as plain as when I saw them with eyes still young. And I can see that something else died there in the bloody mud, and was buried in the blizzard. A people's dream died there. It was a beautiful dream.[24]

The history of the Sioux since Wounded Knee has been less dramatic perhaps, but just as tragic. It has been marked by the slow, deliberate attempt to reduce a free and spirited people to a condition of beggary. The white man has used all his ingenuity and long experience in this attempt. He has starved and imprisoned the Indian. He has pronounced his

[24]Black Elk, as told through John G. Neihardt, *Black Elk Speaks* (Lincoln, Nebraska, 1961), p. 276.

religion illegal. He has forbidden the speaking of the Indian languages.[25] He has, in short, attempted in every conceivable way to strike the death blow to the traditional Indian culture. Yet somehow, the Indian has remained an Indian, clinging desperately and pathetically to the things that have mattered most to him. Despite the years of oppression and neglect, many of the Indian's basic beliefs, values and attitudes have been touched only superficially by those of the whites. Perhaps this stoic endurance constitutes the Indian's victory in defeat and his hope for the future. For even in their darkest hours they have been capable of dignity, faith and humor. If these are enough to sustain a people, then the Sioux will endure.

[25]Jack D. Forbes, ed., *The Indian in America's Past* (Englewood Cliffs, New Jersey, 1964), pp. 113-114. In 1887 the Commissioner of Indian Affairs issued the following order:

"It is believed that if any Indian vernacular is allowed to be taught by missionaries in schools on Indian reservations it will prejudice the pupil as well as his parents against the English language . . . This language which is good enough for a white man or a black man ought to be good enough for the red man. It is also believed that teaching an Indian youth in his own barbarous dialect is a positive detriment to him. The impracticability, if not impossibility, of civilizing the Indians of this country in any other tongue than our own would seem obvious."

INDIAN SINGERS

Harry W. Briton Photo

CHAPTER TWO

The Primitive Imagination and the Purpose of Song

As CONCEIVED by the modern, imagination is the act of forming mental images or concepts of what is not actually present to the senses. The primitive conception of the imagination is quite different, however:

It is resolutely concerned not with what is absent in time or place but what is believed to be present but invisible. So far from creating its subjects out of nothing and making them live in their own authority, it assumes that they exist already and that the singer's task is simply to show what in fact they are, how they work, what is their appearance or character or behavior.[1]

As there are no doubts about the existence, but only the behavior of these invisible presences, they become listed among the *givens* of primitive life. Once these *givens* have been accepted, all things are possible and indeed, often follow quite logically in the primitive mind. Whole orders of being and behavior may then be imagined and accepted. Because the world of the primitive appears to be controlled by supernatural forces, the primitive spends much time and energy in searching for the keys to unlock the mysteries of his physical and spiritual worlds. In the process of doing so, he becomes familiar with the forces imagined to direct the events of the physical world. His task in life as in song then

[1]C. M. Bowra, *Primitive Song* (Cleveland, 1962), p. 206.

(25)

becomes to show what the invisible forces are, how they behave and how they may be approached by the human kind. The primitive grasps these unseen forces with his imagination and brings them into orbit of the commonplace and the familiar. He takes the unseen and the unknown and places them in the more familiar context of the observable and the known.[2]

Of all primitive man's extensive knowledge, the most profound is that of the natural world of which he is a part. This is one of the points of alienation between modern and primitive man. Modern man has, to a great extent, lost his contact with and his reverence for, the natural world. He knows more about nature than at any time in his history, but his immediate contact with nature is probably less than at any time. Modern man has classified nature and has built elaborate scientific orders based on observations and experiment, but he lacks that vital and expanded awareness that characterized the primitive's experience. What modern man lacks is not information about a natural world, but an intensity of feeling for it. To the primitive, who looks through the eyes of the dawn man, the natural world is a place of wonder, familiarity and, paradoxically, mystery. It is a world shared by man, animal and spirit alike, sometimes in harmony, sometimes in conflict. The most common things in the natural world are endowed by the imagination with a power, a personality and a divinity.

The world appears to primitive man neither inanimate nor empty but redundant with life; and life has individuality, in man and beast and plant, and in every phenomenon which confronts man — the thunderclap, the sudden shadow, the eerie and unknown clearing in the wood, the stone which suddenly hurts him when he stumbles while on a hunting trip. Any phenomenon may at any time face him, not as "It," but as "Thou." In this confrontation, "Thou" reveals its individuality, its qualities, its will. "Thou" is not contemplated with intellectual detachment; it is experienced as life confronting life, involving every faculty of man in

[2]Bowra, p. 232.

a reciprocal relationship. Thoughts, no less than acts and feelings, are subordinated to this experience.[3]

The primitive's leap from the natural to the supernatural is not as great as modern man's because it is given an impetus and a justification by his system of logic. The supernatural becomes, for him, an extension of the natural: the unseen becomes an extension of the seen. Even the gods and spirits of the primitive behave in much the same way as men do. Like the gods of Homeric Greece, they become jealous, angry, sullen and remote. Then the primitive may address the spirits as a mother reprimanding a naughty boy: "What are you doing? Where were you when I needed you?" There becomes an easy familiarity between primitive man and the unseen presences which surround him. Once these presences have been accepted, they become a part of that totality of experience with which the primitive lives. In case of such familiarity ". . . the imagination works not so much pictorially but emotionally, not so much by forming a visual image as by catching exactly the right tone for a special occasion."[4]

Though the primitive recognizes a duality between the natural and the supernatural, the two worlds are intimately connected and there is usually a free traffic between them. Spirits roam the natural world, frequently in the disguise of natural beings, and man may enter the spirit world. Many of the primitive's religious and totemistic beliefs are founded on this free association between the worlds of flesh and spirit. Everything in the physical world thus becomes charged with a latent supernatural power that may be used by man to overcome the problems of his environment. At times, without the protective armor of scientific knowledge, these problems appear to overwhelm him and threaten him on all sides. He is usually surrounded by natural enemies, and menaced by starvation, disease and the threat of violent death. His

[3]H. and H. A. Frankfort, John A. Wilson and Thorkild Jacobsen. *Before Philosophy* (Baltimore. 1963), p. 14.

[4]Bowra. p. 209.

only weapons are his intelligence, imagination, skill and magical power. Of these defenses, the most important to him is his *power*. *Power* is the primitive equivalent of what the Greek *New Testament* calls *pneuma,* and what the anthropologists call *mana*:

It is an immaterial and invisible supernatural force, which produces characteristic effects in things influenced by it, and can be transferred from one thing to another under the proper ritual conditions.[5]

Without power, primitive man remains tragically alone and vulnerable, subject to the arrows of Caprice and Chance, the twin devils of the primitive's existence no matter what disguise they assume.

In the search for the power that sustains life and health, the primitive does not distinguish between the subjective and the objective reality of his experience. This does not mean that the primitive ignores reason or even a system of logic as instruments in solving his problems, but it *does* mean that detachment and an objective perspective are inconsistent with the degree of emotional involvement that characterizes his most vital experiences with life. The primitive does not possess science as a way of interpreting experience: such a cold, impersonal calculation of his relationship to the phenomenal world would satisfy neither his animistic sense nor his sense of identification with nature. The "thinking" of the primitive, therefore, is the process which results from his emotional associations with the world as he perceives it. Such a process has been called "emotional thought."[6]

Just as the primitive fails to distinguish between what we would call the objective and the subjective, so he fails to discriminate between what we would consider "reality" and "illusion":

[5]James S. Slotkin, *The Peyote Religion* (Glencoe, Illinois, 1956), p. 69.
[6]H. and H. A. Frankfort, p. 19.

Meaningless, also, is our contrast between reality and appearance. Whatever is capable of affecting mind, feeling, or will has thereby established its undoubted reality. There is, for instance, no reason why dreams should be considered less real than impressions received while one is awake. On the contrary, dreams often affect one so much more than the humdrum events of daily life that they appear to be more, and not less, significant than usual perceptions.[7]

The primitive's first attempt to gain power is usually through the intellect and the imagination. By concentrating his thoughts upon some external reality, the primitive believes that he can influence it in some desired way. He can, for example, by concentrating his thoughts and by focusing his imaginative powers upon the bear, become like the bear, perhaps thereby gaining courage and ferocity in battle. In desert areas where the greatest gift of all is the gift of rain, the primitive's thoughts may dwell constantly on this blessing; all of his imaginative powers may be brought to bear upon it. The primitive believes that such a concentration of power, as well as any ceremonies resulting from it, will aid materially in bringing rain. Modern, scientific man's attempts to seed the clouds present an interesting and a dramatic contrast to the primitive's method, for sophisticated man believes that he can, with varying degrees of success, *control* the forces of nature by the application of scientific laws and procedures. Primitive man believes he can accomplish the same results by the intensity of his thought and the strength of his power. For him, the powers of the mind and the imagination, when combined in a special way, are capable of influencing the conditions of the natural world.

If combined force of concentration and imagination fails the primitive, he must turn to magic, despite all the dangers attendant upon it. He must enter the world of the spirits and find his answers in that nebulous realm. He must become like the wise man in Plato's Allegory and leave the darkness of the cave to begin his solitary journey toward

[7] *Ibid.*, p. 20.

the sun of truth. To find the answers on which his survival often depends he must resort to vision, dream and song. He must cross the boundary of the familiar natural world and explore the terrifying possibilities that may exist elsewhere. Almost all primitive peoples have their way of expanding their consciousness so that it embraces the unknown. The Teton Sioux have long held a rite known as *HaNblecheyapi* or the "vision-seeking quest." The *HaNblecheyapi* is practiced by a young man when he is about to become a hunter and a warrior and requires a power* to protect him from his enemies and make him prosper on the hunt and the warpath. It is the search for a supernatural experience which may also be used by anyone who feels the need for guidance or power from an authority greater than man. First, the votary makes known his desire to conduct such a quest to his family or those closest to him and to a *wicaśa wakaN* or holy man. The *wicaśa wakaN* then outlines the procedures necessary to make the flesh humble and receptive to the revelations from the spirit world. Once these preparatory rites have been properly observed, the young person or person seeking a vision goes off into the hills for his solitary, often four-day vigil. During this period, he eats little or nothing and drinks little water. He spends most of his hours in supplication, crying for a vision. He asks *WakaNtaNka*, the Great Mystery, to take pity on him and he may mutilate and mortify the flesh to dramatize his abject humility in the presence of the Great Mystery. If his quest is successful, he will either enter the spirit world to learn the secret of his power or the spirits will approach him and communicate with him through the familiar things of the natural world. A meadowlark may tell him that it will be is source of power or a wolf may usher him into the spirit world where he may meet a personification or manifestation of *WakaNtaNka* and be charged with a solemn responsibility to his people. Whatever happens, the votary returns to the *wicaśa wakaN*

*The Sioux word for this native power concept is *wowaśke*.

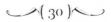

with his vision and asks his mentor to interpret it for him. The holy man may inform him that his power will come from the meadowlark and that he should always treat the bird with reverence and never harm it. The feathers of the meadowlark will then be *wakaN* or sacred and will be an essential part of the votary's medicine bundle, a bundle to be suspended from a tripod before his tipi and which is considered to be the source of his power. Perhaps the young man will relate a song that the meadowlark had sung. If he does, and it is interpreted, then this song becomes another source of his power and his method of communicating with the supernatural world. As the young man goes on the hunt or the warpath, he will sing the song and it will be his power and his strength. He may draw pictographs of the bird and its relation to his vision on his war shield or on the buffalo-hide walls of his tipi. He might even derive his name from the vision and call himself *Zitkala WakaN* or Holy Bird.

What starts with the primitive as a bid for power and understanding ends with song. The song is the final revelation in a quest that began with the imagination confronting some significant problem of the primitive's existence. The song was born of necessity.

Historically, it seems likely that man danced before he sang. The dance is a form of imitative magic that rests on the belief that if man can successfully imitate the animals he hunts or the gods to whom he appeals, then he can bring them under his control. The picture writings of pre-historic man show him dancing in costumes of animal skins and wearing the heads of animals in an attempt to imitate their appearance and behavior. These early dances were probably accompanied by the sounds of primitive percussion instruments, the drum or the rattle. Then human sounds, at first not worthy of the name of language, were used as another part of a ceremonial designed to bring about a specific end. It is probable that these meaningless sounds became a fixed part of the ritual and thereby were assigned some kind of magical value in their own right. Eventually, after thousands of years perhaps, words were assigned meaning and song, as a special and significant use of the language, took its place among the primitive arts. Thus, the word became an important source of power.[9]

It becomes evident then, that song, as composed of meaningful words, is only a part of a ritualistic complex; indeed, it is a relatively recent addition to the matrix that consists of a unity of words, dance and music. Dance and music, however, are the two parts of the complex that are the most vulnerable to time and change. They are the most ephemeral.

But just as we can derive an unusual pleasure from the words of Greek choral song, or *molpe*, of which both the music and the movement are lost, so we can from primitive song. The pleasure is not so complete as it might be if we enjoyed the whole, proper performance, but in isolation the words give the intellectual content of the composite unity. They take us into the consciousness of primitive man at its most excited or exalted or concentrated moments, and they throw a light, which almost nothing else does, on the movements of his mind.[10]

Words are added to music and movement then give to the complex the additional dimension of intellectual power — a power believed to be capable of contributing significantly to the efficacy of the total performance. Words also serve to *explain* and *clarify* dramatic action and have evolved from meaningless adjuncts to an integral part of the matrix. As man attained a higher degree of sophistication, words became more and more important and, as in the case of prayer, came to stand alone without the support of music or movement. Therefore, words alone have become a justifiable, though necessarily incomplete basis for the study of primitive oral expression.

The primitive approaches the word with awe and reverence, and sometimes fear, for the word is conceived to have a creative power of its own. It is not only within the Judeo-

[9]Bowra, pp. 261-263.
[10]*Ibid.*, p. 29.

Christian tradition that ". . . in the beginning was the word."
The primitive imagination also, cannot conceive of creation
from nothingness and so the word is thought to be the first
cause or the prime mover. "It is the thought and the word
that stand face to face with the conscience of the native,
not the deed."[11] The primitive believes that through the
word he can influence and even control the natural and
supernatural forces that appear to direct his life. Among the
Sioux, for example, there are songs known as *Cante Tinza
OlowaN* or Strong Heart Songs. These are the songs of a
society whose purpose is to instill honor and, above all, courage, in the hearts of its members. The words to one of the
songs of the Strong Heart Society are as follows:

kolapi	friends,
tuwa	whoever
nape cinahan	runs away
opa kte śni ye.[12]	shall not be admitted.

In times of crisis and physical danger this song was sung by
its members, either individually or collectively, and it was
believed that a warrior would gain the necessary courage
by singing the words, as though they represented a covenant between the courageous and the source of his power.
Another song whose purpose is close to that expressed in the
Strong Heart Song is this song of encouragement:

akicita	soldiers
nayapapi	you fled;
kiN waNbli kayeś te yelo.[13]	even the eagle dies.

This song hopes to give the singer or his companions courage by recalling that even the eagle, a sacred symbol to the

[11]Margot Astrov, "Editor's Introduction," *American Indian Prose and Poetry* (New York, 1962), p. 3.

[12]Lloyd One Star and singers Ben Black Bear, Iva Black Bear, John Good and Ida White Cow Killer. Recorded by Harry W. Paige in July 1964 at Rosebud, South Dakota; translated by Lloyd One Star.

[13]Densmore, p. 394. *Nayapapi* in 1.2 means "they struck them."

Indians of the Plains, can escape death no more than man and that it is better to die bravely and with honor.

The primitive, through weather incantations, believes that the power of the word may exert an influence on the forces that control the weather, and so songs are composed to concentrate this power on the elements. Bad weather, especially at a major ceremonial, is regarded as a bad omen, a warning by the spirits that the ceremony has incurred their displeasure. Among the Sioux, most significant ceremonies are opened by a song or ritualistic prayer for securing good weather. The song of fair weather is considered to be the reason; the words to the song have the power to insure favorable weather. Songs of healing are sung during or after the administering of special herbs, and the efficacy of the treatment is thought to be as much in the words of the medicine song as in the medicinal value of the potions.

oyate waN waśte nuNwe ca	May the people be good (well); so
waNa piyawakage lo.[14]	life anew I bring you.

Among the Sioux there are even special songs which are used before the treatment of fractures in which the medicine man invokes the power he has received from *mato*, the bear. The healing power of the bear can only be released by the exact combination of words, words which usually come to the medicine man in a dream or vision and thus become the source of his healing power.

To a great extent the primitive's material success in life depends upon the power of his songs. The artistic appeal to the totem[15] becomes as important as the totem itself in bringing about the desired results. Among the Plains Indians material wealth was usually measured by the number and quality of horses that a warrior was able to steal from his

[14]Joseph Thin Elk. Recorded by Harry W. Paige in July 1965 at Mission South Dakota; translated by the writer.

[15]Some writers object to *totem* when used in reference to the culture of the Tetons. As used in this text *totem* means "guardian spirit" or "source of Power."

enemies or capture. Wealth also might be measured by the number of buffalo hides a man could accumulate by his skill as a hunter. The more material possessions a man had the more wives he needed to do the work of preparing the hides and caring for his horses. To attract wives, it was helpful to have the magical power of song. Through song, then, man gains both material wealth and spiritual power.

Although the main purpose of song is power, there are certain songs among the Tetons which might be considered lyrical outbursts — songs of delight in a natural scene or spontaneous utterances of joy or grief. There are also some relatively recent Sioux songs such as the Omaha or Grass Dance Songs which appear to be purely social, the accompaniment to social dancing, but even these, which came from the originally religious Grass Dance Society, were once presented as honor songs intended to celebrate tribal heroes and noble deeds. Even personal songs, often little more than a bald statement of fact by non-Indian standards, may be considered to be oblique attempts to gain power by changing the singer's luck, as this song of discouragement implies:

le waNna henala   Now it is over:
iyotiye kiya   a difficult time
waoN.[16]   I have.

In addition to, and perhaps closely related to the purpose of song as the attainment of power, there are ways in which song is essential to the primitive's survival, fulfilling as it does certain psychological needs. The primitive lives in a mysterious world of which his knowledge is necessarily limited. The entire life cycle is beyond his rational understanding and yet the primitive, like all men, must understand in some way. His songs, because most of them are thought to come from the supernatural, help him to place these mysterious events of the physical world in a context which is meaningful to him. Some of the mystery and therefore the terror of the human condition is diminished by the effect of

[16]Joseph Thin Elk. Recorded by Harry W. Paige in July 1965 at Mission South Dakota; translated by the writer.

song, which is a means of control. Because, in the process of song-making, the primitive is able to put his thoughts and feelings in order, he assumes that the external world too has a corresponding order that he can explain in terms of the supernatural and the magical. This gives him confidence so that he no longer considers himself a helpless victim. The mysteries are brought within his grasp, and by an artistic ordering of words he can impose this order on the physical world which might otherwise appear to be moved by blind forces completely beyond his control. Through song and ritual, the primitive can relate himself and his needs to the structure of an often hostile or indifferent universe.

Song also helps the primitive overcome the fear and the despair which haunt him and, at times, threaten to destroy him. The most compelling of these fears is that he is doomed to extinction. This feeling is most pronounced when the primitive comes into contact with a more advanced society. He has learned from bitter experience that geographical isolation is about his only chance for survival. His enemies are everywhere, and his life is in constant danger. He must usually survive by hunting, and the hunt is a dangerous alternative to starvation. He must protect his hunting grounds and his family from human enemies. He is constantly assailed by the mysterious forces of disease and old age. His songs give him a sense of a continuity of being, and serve to renew and fulfill the mysterious events of the human cycle.

At some undetermined time in the remote past, as stated earlier, words were found to be a part of the complex of dance and music. This addition of meaningful words to ritual was prompted by the belief that the ceremonial complex was somehow incomplete without them and that words, as a source of power, added still another forceful dimension to primitive man's appeal to the supernatural. Since the purpose of this study is to consider these words and the contexts in which they appear as poetry with a purpose, some general characteristics of primitive language as well as certain specific elements of the Lakota language must be examined.

Just as the *purpose* of primitive song is different from that of our own, so the primitive *language* is constructed on different assumptions about the relationship of words to reality. The language of primitive peoples would not be a suitable medium for modern poetry. No primitive language, for example, is adequately equipped with words to convey abstract concepts. It is always the specific that is captured by the primitive imagination and his language has been formed to deal with the specific. In considering the primitive imagination, it has been stated that his imagination is an extension of his observation, that the unseen is but an extension of the seen. Within such a framework there is little need for abstract terms. The primitive also has totems and other manifestations of the supernatural with which he can communicate. In primitive societies the abstract is usually reduced to the specific. It follows then that primitive language is a poor vehicle for conveying abstract concepts and an effective one for dealing with the specific. In the Lakota language there is no abstract term for *animal* or for *liquid*. Even today, with the manifold processes of acculturation well advanced, the older Sioux have no word for motor-driven vehicle, but refer to an automobile as *iyeciNka iNyanke* or "runs by itself."

Though primitive language is weak in abstract terms, its greatest strength is in the number of words rich in impressions of the natural world. The primitive is also able to make fine distinctions, many distinctions relating to objects and happenings in nature. The Eskimo has many words that discriminate between the various kinds of snow — fine, heavy, wet, drifting, etc. The Hopi likewise have a number of words for *rain*, and make similar distinctions like heavy and light, male and female. These distinctions and fine shades of meaning make it necessary for the primitive to have a large vocabulary. The Lakota language contains over thirty thousand words,[17] approximately the same number as Old English, and that fact in itself gives an idea of its richness and effectiveness.

[17] Eugene Buechel, S.J. *A Grammar of Lakota* (St. Louis, 1939), p. 129.

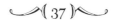

The Lakota language, like most primitive languages, is rich in figurative expression and lends itself well to an impressionistic poetry. Indeed, some Lakota words may be considered to be highly figurative and metaphoric in themselves. The Lakota word for *remember* is *kiksuya* which, literally translated, means to "throw the mind back." The expression for *moon* is *haNhepi wi* or "night sun." The word which expresses our idea of "my heartfelt gratitude" is *chaNtemawaśte* or literally, "you make my heart good." The language itself has a poetic simplicity as will be observed in the following *Wiyośtela OlowaN* or Love Song:

inkpataya nawazin	Up the creek I stand,
na sina cicoze	waving my shawl at you.
maya	Come here!
maya	Come here!
leciya ku waNa.[18]	Hurry to me now!

This poetic simplicity is also seen in the forceful, direct prose of the Plains Indian, a good example of which is the conclusion of Chief Red Cloud's speech at the Cooper Institute in New York City:

I have sent a great many words to the Great Father but they never reached him. They were drowned on the way, and I was afraid the words I spoke lately to the Great Father would not reach you, so I came to speak to you myself; and now I am going away to my home. I want to have men sent out to my people who we know and can trust. I am glad I have come here. You belong in the East and I belong in the West, and I am glad I have come here and that we could understand one another.[19]

The Lakota language is also rich in the expression of personal relationships. Usually men and women use different words to express degrees of relationship within the *tiyośpaye* or extended kinship group. There is, too, a closer relationship within the kinship group than is found among white

[18]Noah Kills-in-Sight. Recorded by Harry W. Paige in August 1965 at Spring Creek, South Dakota; translated by Noah Kills-in-Sight of Spring Creek.

[19]Red Cloud, the *New York Times*, June 17, 1870, Sec. 1, p. 1.

people. The children of a family apply the word *father* (*ate*) both to their real father and to all his brothers, and they are called *children* by them. They also address as *mother* (*ina*) both their real mother and all her sisters, and they are called *children* by them. There are many words in the Lakota language to express these fine distinctions in personal relationships. Often these words are applied to supernatural powers as well: *TuNkasila* or Grandfather may also be used for *WakaNtaNka*, corresponding to the Christian idea of God the Father.

Many Lakota words, when used in a special context, may have esoteric meaning as well. The word *wakaN*, for example, may mean mysterious in the word for gun or firearms which is *mazawakaN* (mysterious iron), or in *mniwakaN*, mysterious water or liquor. The generic word for children is *wakaNheja*, and in this word, the *wakaN* means mysterious also, but more than that: it has here the connotation of something sacred and holy as well. The Lakota word for God, *WakaNtaNka*, cannot be accurately translated, although the whites have captured the spirit of the word if not all the connotations when they translate it as the Great Mystery or the Great Spirit. Frances Densmore gives examples of what she calls the "sacred language" of the Teton Sioux. She explains this language as a necessary tool ". . . in order that persons intimate with supernatural things could communicate without being understood by the common people."[20] The expression *yatin kte*, literally "you will eat," is a phrase used only by medicine men when addressing the sick. The word *tunkaN* is supposed to be derived from *tuNkasila*, grandfather, and it means "sacred stones." The phrase "in a sacred manner," used in so many of the religious songs of the Sioux, cannot be regarded as an accurate or adequate rendering of the original *wakaN yaN*.[21]

Even though much of the primitive's poetical inspiration is unconscious, his art is conscious. As his songs are really

[20]Densmore, p. 120.
[21]*Ibid.*

prayers for supernatural assistance, he feels that they must be exact and precise in every way, both in composition and in performance. Songs must be artistically ordered if they are to produce the desired results, and the primitive spends much time in finding the exact word and placing it in the exact context. Song may be power, but power is also potentially dangerous. This explains the fact that there is so little change in primitive song and ritual; it helps explain the basic conservatism of the primitive. As songs are often thought to be derived from supernatural inspiration or intervention, they cannot be changed or revised without endangering their efficacy and magical power. The primitive is often reluctant to tell outsiders of his songs for much the same reason. He feels that in revealing his songs to someone else, he puts himself in a vulnerable position because they could be turned against him. Mistakes in song and ritual may be equally as dangerous, and the primitive makes every effort to insure that they are faithfully executed.

The word, then, is held close to the heart of the native and is considered to be a gift of the supernatural powers, though it may appear to be no more than a statement of fact. The forces of inspiration behind the creative process are regarded as mysterious and inexplicable, but the songs, in most cases, are specific and clear both in purpose and in method to those familiar with the culture. The imagination works on the mysterious and puts it in terms of the familiar and then presents it to the supernatural as a plea or prayer for power and control. Song-making may be considered to be the process by which the mysterious and the holy are made understandable and pragmatic. The song is the native's prayer for power to preserve and to live his life.

CHAPTER THREE

The Nature of Primitive Song

THE PURPOSE of primitive song is power, and power may mean almost anything that man believes he cannot attain by and for himself. Considered as such, primitive song has no limitations as to its purpose: the appeal may be made for the power to destroy enemies, the power to recover from illness or wounds, the power to lead a healthy, happy life, the power to attract the opposite sex, and the power for the people to survive as a nation. Milton's conception of the poet as priest and prophet would surprise no one in a primitive society, just as his avowed intention in *Paradise Lost* — to justify God's ways to man — would have been considered a legitimate poetic task to the primitive, if *justify* were interpreted to mean *explain*. Milton's high seriousness of purpose would also have been endorsed by the primitive as the proper attitude for the work of the creative imagination. The primitive singer is a priest of the natural world, and the rainbow that spans the heavens and earth is his altar.

Though the purpose of primitive song may be unlimited, the subject is limited to the particular. Though the primitive's appeal may be universal, it is made in terms of the particular and through the particular. This results, in part, from the primitive's indifference to the abstract and his intimate knowledge of the familiar forms in the narrow, restricted world in which he lives. It also results from his tendency to refuse to make distinctions between the natural and the supernatural. In a sense, the primitive approaches the supernatural like the juggler of Notre Dame, with his familiar phrases and bids for power aloft and in delicate balance.

Primitive song has certain general characteristics. One of these is the knowledge that it assumes about the circumstances of its composition. There are few secrets in a society in which its members live together in close physical contact. If a wife is having an affair with another man, it is well known to all the members of the tribe or band. Her infidelity may solicit a variety of individual reactions, and even perhaps some songs of ridicule, but her unfaithfulness is no secret. If a man sings a song of discouragement, he is not expected to include the circumstances which led to its composition. The reasons for his discouragement, and the degree of it, would be well known to the listeners. Primitive life is characterized by an infinite repetition of common experiences. There is not a great opportunity for variety of experience, even though there may be many individual responses to experience. The same problems are faced by all in the communal life. Even the chief does not prosper if the people do not. In song, then, there is a lack of revealed background that seems to remove it from its dramatic setting.

The bare simplicity of existence accounts for the repetition of conventional themes, but this does not dull their relevance or fall below the proper level of song. It means rather that variations on them are always relevant and in some sense new.[1]

The following begging song, for example, represents the very least that might have been said:

pejuta sapa	Coffee (black medicine)
waciN ye	I want.
aguyapi	Bread
waciN ye.[2]	I want.

In this song, the singer does not relate the circumstances of his poverty like the beggar on the city streets with his down-

[1]Bowra. p. 95.

[2]Noah-Kills-in-Sight. Recorded by Harry W. Paige in August 1965 at Spring Creek, South Dakota; translated by the writer.

on-my-luck story. The circumstances behind the fact are already known to all. What matters most is food and drink, and a sentimental appeal would be redundant since the members of the tribe or band would know without being informed, that it is the responsibility of those who have food to share it with those who do not. There is no need for either explanation or entreaty, but only a *pilamiye*, or thank you. The song is functionally perfect, and so, to the primitive, artistically perfect as well. The primitive singer, because he shares the communal life, also assumes that what interests him, interests all. Tragedy and joy are not secrets of the heart, and neither are the singer's reactions to them.

Many primitive songs seem concerned with the trivial and the insignificant, by sophisticated standards. Indeed, one of the characteristics of the primitive imagination is that it grasps what often seems to be inconsequential and magnifies it. The Winter Counts, highly personalized pictographs drawn on buffalo or deer hide and representing the event for which a particular year is remembered, are replete with examples of this. The year of the Custer fight, 1876, is depicted on the Big Missouri Winter Count as The Winter That the Sioux Smoked the Pipe with the Omaha, an event of far more significance to Big Missouri than the Custer defeat. In other Winter Counts one may look in vain for reference to a great event in the white man's history and find instead that the year may be known as the winter that somebody lost his best horse. This apparent concern for the insignificant is also evident in the names that are given to places. Wounded Knee, for example, was so named because a Sioux hunter accidently shot himself in the knee while hunting in that area. The Upper Cut Meat Creek District on the Rosebud Reservation has that name because it was once the place where government meat rations were issued to the Indians. In the physical proximity of communal living, the apparently commonplace takes on an added dimension and appeals to the interest and imagination of all. The usual becomes one of the common denominators of primitive life.

Primitive song is born of necessity and so has a sense of immediacy and urgency. There is, of course, an urgency about primitive life and the harsh conditions it imposes on man. The hunt must be successful or the people go hungry. The enemy must be slain or the primitive's family may be destroyed. There are demands on the hunter and the warrior that nothing short of success will meet. As most songs are, in a larger sense, songs for survival, they resemble prayer. The ends of magic and prayer are identical, though the appeal may be presented differently. Magic attempts to coerce the supernatural powers, while prayer tries to bring about its end by entreaty and supplication.[3] The following song, sung by Sioux medicine man, Two Shields, illustrates this sense of immediacy and urgency:

aNeptu mitawa koN	May this be the day which
letu nuNwe	I considered mine;
waziyata	from the north
tate uye ciN	the wind is blowing.
aNpetu mitawa koN	May this be the day which
letu nuNwe.[4]	I considered mine.

This is a discouragement song, sung when the singer ". . . was worried or disappointed."[5] It is also a plea for power, invoking the northern cardinal point as intercessor. The tone is one of urgency and very close to prayer. In another song, a warrior, perhaps beyond the years of fighting, is advised to "settle down." There is a persistent, nagging urgency about this song, and one may easily imagine a worried woman as the singer. Yet the tone is also respectful: there is no mention of age or wounds or cowardice.

---

[3]John Greenway, *Literature among the Primitives* (Hatboro, Pennsylvania, 1964), p. 53.

[4]Densmore, p. 277.

[5]*Ibid.*, p. 276.

zuyapi kiN he	going on the warpath
ayuśtaN	you should give up
na	and
owaNzila yaNke	settle down
waciN	you should desire
na	and
ataNsela	stop
hecel yaNka na[6]	for good.

This sense of urgency and simple directness gives primitive song a childlike innocence and a sense of wonder and discovery. Primitive man looks at life through the eyes of the innocent. He lives in a world that has not been classified, explained away, or reduced to formulae. He moves in a world of infinite possibility.

Primitive song has general formal characteristics which serve to identify and explicate it. It is both oral and dramatic. From the brief outline of words which represents primitive song in its written form, this is not always apparent. The reader must therefore elaborate on the skeletal structure presented to him. In this respect, primitive song is like the Japanese tradition of Haiku, demanding that the reader be a creator as well. Primitive song is oral because there is not a written tradition among primitives and because it is usually a part of a greater complex of music, song and dance. It is dramatic because it is the acting out of a segment of a myth or a ritual. Singing and storytelling, and most combinations thereof, are by their very nature, dramatic events. They usually require an audience, or participators, and though the words of the song are usually brief, they are repeated often and are accompanied by the imitative magic of the dance or by some form of dramatic accompaniment.

Even a ritual song consisting of four lines will be repeated many times and it will be accompanied by a dramatic performance in which each word conjures up some form of dramatic action. In many of the Sioux songs of healing, for example, *mato*, the bear, is thought to be responsible for the

[6]*Ibid.*, p. 374. The *waciN* in 1.5 should be *yaciN*.

efficacy of the herbs or brews administered to the patient. This is the reason why the bear is held in such high esteem by the Sioux and many other tribes of the Plains. In fact, among the Sioux, the bear is usually the animal that appears in dreams to give to man roots and herbs with curative powers. This explains why so many Sioux names are derived from the bear and why it was once considered a great feat to count *coup* on him. The bear is dangerous, of course, but the Sioux also consider him kind to reveal the secrets of healing to man. In songs of healing, the medicine man or bear doctor, imitates the bear in his dramatic presentation which accompanies song. He dresses in the skin of a bear, paints his face, and imitates the sounds and the actions of the bear. The Sioux, like most primitive peoples, once lived intimately with the "four leggeds" of the animal world and knew much about their actions and habits. A bear doctor, especially, will study the animal carefully as it appears in reality or dream, in order to discover its ways and habits, and so make his own power more effective. A healing song by a bear doctor may last for hours and show an understanding of that animal quite beyond the comprehension of modern, sophisticated man. The following is a song of healing in which the singer traces the origin of his power to a dream in which he was given certain roots and herbs by the bear itself:

pezihuta waN	a medicine
yatin kte	you will eat;
kahantu	at that place
naziN ye	it stands.
mato	A bear
hemakiye.[7]	said this to me.

The song is brief and without ornamentation, and by itself gives no idea of the dramatic complex in which a primitive man pits all his magical skill against death. The reader of these lines does not hear the groans of the victim or the harsh punctuations of the gourd rattles. He does not hear

[7]Densmore, p. 196. *Pezihuta* in 1.1 should be *pejuta*, *naziN* in 1.4 should be *najin yelo*, and *mato* in 1.5 should be followed by the article *waN*.

the torn and mournful keening of relatives. The reader does not see in his mind's eye the crazy geometry of shadow thrown by the fire on the sides of the tipi. He does not hear the medicine man as he cries to the bear to intercede, calling him *ate* or *father* as well as *mato*. Only the informed imagination can appreciate the drama involved in it.

A song may be solo or choral, but in either case the singer does not consider it the product of his own creative imagination. This is why practically all primitive songs are thought to be anonymous. The singers among the contemporary Sioux will usually say that the song was given to them by their father, grandfather, or some other relative, or else that it came to him in a dream or vision. Song, as the appeal for power, is regarded as a gift from supernatural powers. This gift may come through a natural agent such as the bear, the elk, or the sacred stones, or it may come directly through the supernatural as it does in visions in which a mortal may be taken into the spirit world to learn of its secrets. Individual or solo songs are obtained from someone, usually a relative or else are given to the singer by the supernatural or its natural agents. Such songs are considered to be the property of the individual, and a primitive copyright protects his songs. Presumably, his song would not be of any great value to someone else and might even represent a potential danger.

Magic, like explosives, must be treated with care. Songs of the individual could, however, be given to another person along with the circumstances of its composition. In this way, the new owner would know the source of his newly-acquired power and the rites necessary for its continued effectiveness. Such individual songs would include love songs, discouragement songs, songs of spirits, strong heart songs and the like. Choral or group songs would be those used as a part of the ritual and ceremonial or those representing the songs of societies. These songs usually call for the participation of the entire body eligible for such participation, and are often highly dramatic and accompanied by music and dance.

Primitive song is designed and ordered according to the primitive's artistic standards. To the casual observer, however, it may seem fragmentary, disordered, and without artistic merit of any kind. The primitive is conservative and Custom is usually one of his gods. His life and goods are threatened constantly by the hostile or indifferent forces of his environment. In order to compensate for the disorder in his life, he is forced to impose an order upon external events. This imposed order is the only security he can ever know, and so it must be included in all of his artistic endeavors — in the strict geometric design of his graphic arts as well as in his ritual and song. Most rituals, for example, have been passed down under the strict dictates of Custom, and have not changed substantially since their inception. Every part of the ritual has its special purpose and manner of execution, down to the most minute detail. No part of the ritual may be altered in the slightest way without threatening the intention of the ritual or turning it into a complete disaster.

Among the contemporary Sioux, the older people are frequently openly critical of the failure to observe all the complexities of older rituals like the Sun Dance. They feel that if the cottonwood tree which will serve as the Sun Dance pole is not first struck by a virgin of spotless reputation, then any potentially good results of the whole ceremony will be nullified. The Sioux have a strong sense of imminent justice, and sometimes the older people will have premonitions of disaster because the Sun Dance Director, through carelessness or indifference, had made serious mistakes in conducting the ceremony. The strict observance of ritualistic procedures, then, is one way of imposing an order on things mysterious. The following song is an example of a song that attempts to bring a discernible order to the lives of all the members of the nation:

lenake	all these
waku wapi kte	move with a purpose,
lenake	all these
waku wapi ktelo	move with a purpose;

tuNkaN oyate waN	a sacred-stone nation
waku wapi kte	moves with a purpose;
lenake	all these
waku wapi ktelo.[8]	move with a purpose.

One of the most obvious characteristics of primitive song is its brevity. Certainly, it is designed to extract the greatest possible meaning from each word, denotatively as well as connotatively. One old Sioux, when questioned about the brevity of his songs, replied: "The songs are short because we know a lot." This remark was not made in a spirit of humor or conceit. It was simply a statement of fact. So many of the circumstances of its composition and rendition would be known that it would be redundant to offer them; hence such details are excluded from primitive song because the listeners or the spirits to whom it is addressed would already know them. Songs may be brief also because they appear within the context of a story: their function is to serve as a dramatic emphasis of the significant point. The Sioux have a one-line song called *SuNka OlowaN* or the Song of the Dog Feast:

SuNka wayataniN![9]   Feast well, O dog!

This song appears meaningless in its brevity and cryptic reference until it is set in its proper narrative place. Long ago the Sioux were starving and so they went hunting near the Black Hills. They had little luck and, in their desperation, vowed that they would give their dogs a great feast if they helped find the buffalo. Soon after this vow was made, they saw a great herd and the people killed many. But, before they ate, they remained faithful to their vow. They placed the choicest cuts of meat in the center of a circle. Then, they painted their dogs with red stripes, in a ceremonial manner. They held the dogs while they sang three times: *SuNka wayataniN!* With the third rendition they released the dogs to devour the meat. After that, the people

[8]Densmore, p. 221.
[9]*The Indians' Book,* ed. Natalie Curtis (New York, 1923), p. 59.

ate. This was the beginning of the Dog Feast, a custom that was once regarded as *wakaN,* that is, holy, mysterious and full of power for the people.[10]

Another cause of brevity in primitive song is that stock phrases are used, phrases that are known to all the members of the social unit. In the songs of the Sioux, we find such stock phrases as *ho u wayin kte* (a voice I will send), *kola wayelo* (is my friend), *niwakaN* (may you be sacred), and *wakaNyan* (in a sacred manner). These stock phrases or formulae are an important part of composition that puts no special premium on originality, but rather evoke many stock responses by a few stock phrases. Such phrases, because they are well known to the audience, contribute significantly to the brevity of the song. The people can react to the phrases without the singer's elaboration. It is a convenient system of shorthand which eliminates the need for a more formal development of an incident or an idea. Used in this way, stock phrases may be likened to the slang of our popular songs. When a popular singer laments the fact that his "baby left" and now he's "blue," we understand both the situation and his reaction to it. He has set the stage for us in a few, well-chosen words. To the imaginative and the sophisticated, cliches may be the stale choices of an impoverished imagination, but they are the substance of popular literature and song. The cliche of idea or language evokes the necessary response of the audience for whom it is presented. In this respect, then, it is effective communication.

In addition to stock phrases, a secret, sacred language produces brevity in primitive song in a different way. These sacred phrases contribute to brevity by suggesting the unknown and mysterious and by evoking one of many possible responses to the singer's words, depending on the audience's awareness of the circumstances of composition or the appeal made. The sacred language has a multiplicity of meanings, and though references are brief, they are still concerned with magic and therefore elicit a powerful, though often inarti-

[10]*The Indians' Book,* pp. 58-59.

culate response. Sometimes it becomes necessary for an *itancaN* (leader) or a shaman to communicate with the supernatural in such a way that the communication remains secret. A shaman and bear doctor who has received his knowledge of healing from *mato,* the bear, might use the expression *yatin kte,* literally, "you will eat," an expression used ceremonially only in the magical context of the healing song.

The phrase, *maka cokataN* or "at the center of the earth," is still another example of a sacred expression used by those whose special training or experience has allowed them to engage in magic. Even the word *wakaN* is a part of this sacred language because of the multiplicity of its levels of meaning — holy, mysterious, sacred, wonderful, and incomprehensible. Another part of this secret language is the silence between renditions of the song. Just as the rest is a part of the music, so the silence is a part of the song. Some songs are introduced by a perceptible silence that may serve as a prelude to its serious purpose, in the way that the Quakers and other sects may wait in silence for the "still, small voice." That which is not stated, but understood, permits the song to be brief and, at the same time, meaningful. For the Sioux, silence represents that perfect state of equilibrium of spiritual perfection in which all tensions are resolved. Dr. Charles Eastman, whose Dakota name was *Ohiyesa,* considers this respect for silence as one of the most significant characteristics of the Indian:

He believes profoundly in silence — the sign of a perfect equilibrium. Silence is the absolute poise or balance of body, mind, and spirit. The man who preserves his selfhood is ever calm and unshaken by the storms of existence — not a leaf, as it were, astir on the tree; not a ripple upon the surface of the shining pool — his, in the mind of the unlettered sage, is the ideal attitude and conduct of life.[11]

[11]Charles A. Eastman, *From the Deep Woods to Civilization* (Boston, 1916). p. 156.

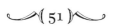

In the *HaNblecheyapi* or vision-seeking quest, the votary
seeks to meditate on things *wakaN* in solitude and in silence.
It may be said paradoxically that, among the Sioux, silence
is the most profound form of communication with the spiritual powers, and is therefore a significant part of their songs
and tends to make the words fewer. Another device which
serves the cause of brevity is the use of meaningless vocables.
In the ritual of the Native American Church or the Peyote
Cult, there is a curious blending of Christian doctrine and
native elements. Meaningless vocables are alternated with
the spelling of the name J-E-S-U-S in at least one song and
such variation is used to help create the hypnotic atmosphere that dominates the cult meetings. These meaningless
vowel sounds are also used for the artistic effect of balanc-
ing a line.

Primitive song achieves its formal unity by construction
around a single idea, incident, or theme. Primitive man deals
with only one thing at a time — in life and in song. Once
the single theme is stated, the variations on it follow, the
number of these variations often determining the length of
the song. The following is a brief song about a dream and its
effect on the dreamer:

Cetan Hota	Gray Hawk
miye.	I am.
Wahi.[12]	I come.

In this case, the incident is the receiving of a dream of the
hawk and the taking of the totem's name. The idea also
contributes to the unity: by adopting the name of the bird-
spirit, the possessor will gain some of the power associated
with it. The song is repeated in four sets of four repetitions,
invoking the four cardinal points and so insuring the presence of the Great Mystery.

Primitive song also uses conventional poetic devices, but
with purposes somewhat different from those of modern
verse. Perhaps the most important of these is repetition, for

[12]Joseph Thin Elk. Recorded by Harry W. Paige in July 1965 at Mission,
South Dakota; translated by the writer

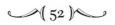

through its magical use power is increased and power, as explained in Chapter Two, is almost the sole purpose of primitive song. Also, repetition calms the primitive's fears and gives him a sense of mastery over the word — and what the word stands for. What is repeated becomes familiar, and even if it is not fully understood it still gives reassurance by its very familiarity. What is repeated becomes familiar, and what is familiar is not as threatening. Words are repeated; phrases are repeated; stanzas are repeated; and songs are repeated to gain power. Oftentimes, repetition with an increment is used. Repetition leads naturally to variation and variation to parallelism. Parallelism is, in fact, a more complicated application of repetition and usually adds something to the theme, frequently in the form of paradox. In the following song, designed to bring success on the buffalo hunt in time of famine, there has been a new dimension added by the use of parallelism.

canonNpa waN	A pipe
caze yal	they mentioned
manipi	as they walked;
ota	many times
eyahpeya	I have offered this
mawani	as I walked.
maka śa waN	A red earth
caze yal	they mentioned
manipi	as they walked;
ota	many times
icaḫtak	it has been placed upon me
mawani	as I walked.
makato waN	A blue earth
caze yal	they mentioned
manipi	as they walked;
ota	many times
icaḫtak	it has been placed upon me
mawani.[13]	as I walked.

[13]Densmore, p. 445. *Caze* in 1.2 should be *caje* and *mawani* in 1.6 should be *wamani*. These changes would apply in all three stanzas.

In the ceremony which accompanied this song, a buffalo skull was painted blue and red, representing earth and sky, and set beside a sacred pipe, filled and resting on a bed of sage. As a result of the singing of this song and the ceremony, performed in darkness, the buffalo skull was believed to come alive and call other buffalo near the camp where they could be hunted.[14] The artistic effect, and no doubt a part of the magical effect desired, rests on its unity, repetition, and parallelism.

Rhyme, one of the most important of European poetic devices, is almost wholly absent from primitive song, and where it does appear, it is usually accidental. Herbert J. Spinden summarizes this point effectively:

The outstanding feature of American Indian verse construction comes from parallel phrasing, or, let us say, repetition with an increment, which gives an effect not of rhyming sounds but of rhyming thoughts.[15]

Alliteration, another familiar device of primitive song, is seen in the preceding song. In the first stanza there is an intentional repetition of the *ch* sound in *canonNpa* and *caze* as well as a repetition of the *ma* sound in the verbal forms *manipi* and *mawani*.

Personification is a device which occurs frequently in primitive song. The primitive believes that many things in the natural world are manifestations of a divinity, and that these have the power to communicate with man. In a world of unlimited possibility, it is not surprising that animals and natural objects may have the power of speech. The primitive accepts this idea with all the ease of a child listening to animals speak in the animated cartoon. The following song illustrates the singer's uncritical acceptance of the white eagle's "voice" as delivering intelligible "speech":

[14]*Ibid.*, p. 444.
[15]Herbert J. Spinden, *Songs of the Tewa* (New York, 1933), p. 58.

waNmayaNka yo	"Regard me!"
WaNbli Ska waN	A white eagle
hemakiya	said to me.
ho	"A voice
hiyuwaye.[16]	I send"

Even today, many of the older Sioux can give extensive accounts of their communication with the supernatural powers through creatures and objects of the natural world.

The imagery of the primitive is expressed in terms of natural objects and actions. Despite the fact that the Sioux live, and have lived, in close contact with nature, they do not usually draw on the nature about them for their imagery in song. The mountains, the grass and flowers seldom appear as images in their art. C. M. Bowra has stated well the use of imagery in primitive song:

Primitive peoples use images, which are not, like most of our own, literary devices to stress one or another aspect of a subject, but a means to make sense of what is otherwise hard to grasp. They are the elementary stuff of myth and are taken quite literally, even if it is recognized that their present function is not quite the same as in more commonplace spheres of action.[17]

To "make sense of what is otherwise hard to grasp" is roughly equivalent to the gaining of power, for explanation is of no particular value to the primitive without the opportunity for control. In the songs of the Sioux, as in most primitive song, imagery is presented in terms of the elements which can bring power to the singer. Among the Sioux, imagery in song is usually the language of power and its metaphoric equivalents. The four elements and the cardinal points, frequently mentioned in song, represent the manifestations of the Lakota gods: Sun, Earth, Sky and the Directions. As additional evidence of the power concept, it will be observed that Wind is frequently used in place of the traditional element, Air. The two are not the same, for Wind

[16]Noah Kills-in-Sight. Recorded by Harry W. Paige in August 1965 at Spring Creek, South Dakota; translated by the writer.

[17]Bowra, p. 209.

is Air in motion, and it is the motion that is capable of bearing men, disease, and such a terrible natural phenomenon as the tornado. These gods are also associated with one of the four cardinal points as well as a color. It is from these sources of power that the imagery of the Tetons is drawn. The fact that flowers or mountains do not appear as images in song does not necessarily mean that the Indian is insensitive to beauty around him, but it does mean that the imagery of his songs concentrates primarily on power, that is, natural forces. A Sioux man might give flowers, trade cloth or a horse to his love, but his song would be concerned with how he might win magical power over her.

Symbolism is an important part of primitive song and may be divided into two distinct, but related types — private and public. Private symbolism is employed in those songs or lines in which the singer would share his meaning with no one but the spiritual powers. The sacred or *wakaN* language of the Sioux, already noted as one of the causes of brevity in their songs, is also highly symbolic and represents a deliberate attempt to keep its meaning a secret lest its magical efficacy be diminished or lost. Thus, an individual may keep his song to himself by means of this private symbolism, as he was sometimes directed to do by the spirit that gave him the song. Public symbolism would be recognized by all members of the social unit. The colors, the directions, and the elements all have a symbolic value, not only in the graphic arts, but also in song. There are many references to them in symbolic terms.

Allusion is also used in primitive song, and it is both a poetic device and a cultural stimulant. There are many allusions in Sioux song to what is believed to be the earliest of all sacred happenings, the coming of the White Buffalo Maiden and her gift of the sacred pipe.[18] Allusion is also used as metaphor, a way of making meaningful connections through language. The word for sacred stone is *tuNkan*, an abbreviated form of *tuNkaśila*, which is itself an allusion to *WakaN-*

18Densmore, p. 78.

taNka as Grandfather. Many of the metaphors and figures of speech are presented in the form of allusion. Culturally, allusion is a way of passing tradition from one generation to another and thus keeping the old ways alive in the minds and hearts of the young people.

JOSEPH THIN ELK, SINGER

—*Harry W. Paige Photo.*

CHAPTER FOUR

Individual Songs

SOLO SONGS are different from choral songs in that they represent an individual interpretation of experience rather than a collective response. The Sioux Indian is both a fervent individualist and a dedicated conformist to the group, and he sees no Emersonian contradiction in his position. In the popular imagination such chiefs as Red Cloud and Spotted Tail were men of unlimited political power, the great war lords of the Plains, who represented a centralized authority. In actual fact, the Sioux never had a head chief until one was appointed by the officials in Washington, who hoped that it might be easier to deal with one responsible individual, preferably one who would be willing to see things from the white man's point of view. In the almost pure democracy of the Plains Indian, the chiefs of a band or *tiyóspaye* ruled by the consent of the people and the strength of his character and personality alone. The Sioux owed no allegiance to any man because he bore a title. This fierce individualism of the Sioux caused much misunderstanding among the whites, and even among some Indians.

When the Black Hills were "sold" by the Sioux, the incident split the people as few things had done up to that time. Most Indians asked the obvious question: How could the chiefs sell what was not theirs? By whose authority could such a betrayal be perpetrated? Crazy Horse, Big Foot, Sitting Bull, and other chiefs branded as "hostiles" by the government, simply refused to recognize the "sale" as binding on the Sioux "Nation." Indeed, for most of the Sioux, there was no Sioux "Nation," but only a theoretical whole made up of its parts, mostly bands or camps such as those of the Oglala, who met once a year at Sun Dance time for their mutual interest and satisfaction. The Sioux recognized no one who spoke for all of them — not even Red Cloud at the height of his glory. In warfare, also, the Sioux warrior fought as an individual. As the most important part of war was not killing the enemy, but winning individual distinction, it was usually a case of every man for himself, a strategy that made the Indian poorly equipped to fight according to the white man's concept of war. Yet, despite the individualism of the Sioux, he *was* subject to custom and tradition, as explained by Luther Standing Bear:

The Lakota word for this governing power of custom or tradition was *wouncage*, literally, "our way of doing." *Wouncage* constituted, for the Lakota people, the only authority.[1]

It was difficult for any individual, no matter how independent, to break away from *wouncage* and all that the word implied. The solo songs of the Sioux reflect this dual allegiance to the Self and to the social unit of which he was a part. Songs of praise will often be highly individualistic by primitive standards and, at the same time, will observe *wouncage*. In hunting songs, the individual may praise himself extravagantly for his courage and skill, but usually the *I* dissolves into *we* and the singer concludes with ". . . food I give away." A contemporary song, sung at a benefit or Giveaway for a family whose home had burned down, illustrates the same spirit:

Wahpanice kiN ota	The poor are many,
ca	so
talo na woyute	meat and food
wana wecoN welo.[2]	I give away now.

[1] Luther Standing Bear, *Land of the Spotted Eagle* (Boston, 1933), p. 124. Lest this brief quotation imply otherwise, the Sioux were not without forms of coercion, especially by the camp police during times when it was necessary to maintain strict order.

[2] John Good. Recorded by Harry W. Paige in July 1964 at Rosebud, South Dakota; translated by the writer.

Because of the nature and brevity of Sioux songs, there is no such thing as personal style or formal mannerisms as we think of them. It is impossible to recognize an unperformed song as Sitting Bull's or Red Cloud's in the way that we might recognize a poem as the work of Thomas Hardy or A. E. Housman. In the complete absence of a written tradition, it is the rendition that is all important. The singer is first of all, a performer, and whatever individual style the song has is in its performance. The performance may convey more than the words. The words of solo songs do, however, tell something of the singer: they reflect his imagination, his characteristic attitudes, and his powers of articulation. They tell whether he loves or ridicules the woman of whom he sings. They tell whether he is discouraged and pessimistic or whether he is hopeful and confident. It is quite probable that some solo songs represent a lyrical outburst inspired by love or natural beauty, or even by the sheer delight in being alive.

One beautiful summer day, near the community of Wounded Knee on the Pine Ridge Reservation, the writer saw an old man sitting cross-legged on the prairie stubble before his log shack. He was alone, a frail Buddha-like figure set against the vast emptiness of the plains. Suddenly, he lifted his cracked voice in song, repeating this simple lyric again and again:

le aNpetu   This day
waśte.[3]   is good.

Another time, when the writer visited Joseph Thin Elk in his isolated cabin north of Mission, South Dakota, he found the old man near his *initi* or Sweat Lodge, singing this greeting to the morning star:

[3]Song by an unknown singer; collected and translated by Harry W. Paige.

wi he napa caN
WakaNtaNka onkeyela on hena wicaḫpi
waNkal okawinga ci
oyate kiN le wihiNapa ke el wopila
onke niciyapi.[4]

The sun comes up:
it is next to the Great Mystery, the
morning star.
The people give thanks that the sun
comes up this day.

Songs like these are not easy to classify because it is difficult
to tell whether they are mere spontaneous reactions or cryptic, even subconscious forms of magical appeal.

Where the distinction can be made, individual songs are
usually secular rather than religious. In pre-reservation days,
as today, songs were usually spoken of as being "given" to
the singer by some agent, either natural or supernatural. The
Sioux seldom regards himself as a creator of song, but only
as the successful recipient of its power. Even a love song
might come to him from the elk (believed to have special
powers to influence the course of human love) and represents a source of magical power over the loved one.

wicayaka hecina yaoN śni   If you are faithful, come!
heḫaka WaN   An elk
waNlaka nuNwe.[5]   may you see.

Whatever their source of inspiration, solo songs are considered the prize of the individual rather than the group,
and may be classified as secular in the sense that they do not
represent a concerted, ritualistic drama designed for a
specific end.

Solo songs also cover a wide range of subject matter, and
every phase of the human cycle and condition is included in
their spectrum. The events of the human cycle have always

[4]Joseph Thin Elk. Recorded by Harry W. Paige in July 1965 at Mission,
South Dakota; translated by James E. Emery of Rapid City, South Dakota.

[5]John Good. Recorded by Harry W. Paige in July 1964 at Rosebud, South
Dakota; translated by the writer.

been a source of the greatest mystery and sacredness to the Sioux, and call for the most intense of emotional responses. These reactions are then put in the form of song, depending on what events are considered most significant in the culture. It is characteristic of the primitive that his reservoir of emotions overflows at frequent intervals. Though he may appear to be stoical to the outsider, he is, in fact, emotionally demonstrative within his group. The writer has attended wakes in full-blood communities that were positive orgies of grief. Women mourners had slashed off their long hair so it hung ragged and matted. Some had cut their arms and legs with knives, allowing the clotted blood to remain as a badge of their sorrow.[6] Other women keened a mournful dirge that pierced like a blade and set the nerves vibrating. The events of the human cycle are attended with many dangers. The act of giving birth is not only *wakaN;* it is also dangerous in a society in which magic is often more important than science. Even menstruation represents a threat, particularly to the efficacy of magical rites.

One old Indian in the Rosebud Public Health Service Hospital left at the insistence of a medicine man and friend who visited him because a nurse in attendance was menstruating. Disease is a source of terror to people who know practically nothing of the germ theory, and even today, the older and more isolated Sioux are reluctant to go to the hospital for fear they will "never get out again." It is a common occurrence for some of the older, frightened Indians to steal away from the hospital at the first opportunity, a practice that brands them as "skippers" in the eyes of the hospital officials. In contrast to the hospital experience, illness in a traditional community can be something of a social occasion: friends and relatives visit the patient; the pipe is carried to the medicine man to summon him, and, before long, the air is filled with the sounds of drum, rattle and song. Although the curative value of such practices has yet to be demonstrated, it is probably true that, for the old Indian who lies

[6]This practice of cutting the limbs is most unusual today, although it was common in older times.

alone and ill, the sight of his friends and relatives and their obvious concern for him, may be as therapeutic as the clinically dispassionate treatment of the white "pill man."

Generally, though, old age and its accompanying physical decline are anticipated with dread in a culture which has always placed a high premium on physical prowess. Death is lived with on intimate terms, and its shadow is always present. All these events of the human cycle elicit powerful emotional responses which are channeled into song, usually individual rather than ceremonial. There is, for example, no regular ceremony designed to introduce or bless the new born. Such a sacred event would be celebrated in song, but in an individual rather than a ceremonial way. The birth of a child, though feared as dangerous, has long been regarded as the greatest gift from *WakaNtaNka*, and birth is considered *wakaN*, in all its multiplicity of meanings. It is significant that there are no birth songs recorded by students of the Sioux. Not even the scholarly work of Frances Densmore contains a single birth song. It would be logical to conclude then, that such songs were highly personalized expressions of joy, and assumed no ritualistic format. The writer asked one of his informants about this and was told that sometimes the traditional Sioux sing a simple birth song upon the arrival of a child. He then proceeded to sing the song that he had composed when his first son had been born:

ciNks bluha	A son I have;
nuNwe icaNte tiNza yelo	may his heart be strong!
mazaska	Money
wecon welo.[7]	I donated.

It is interesting to note that, while there are no ceremonies to celebrate the birth of a child, there is a beautiful ceremony by which the parents demonstrate their love for the child by presenting him with a "second father," or, more often, serves as a means of binding children to children in

[7]Lloyd One Star. Recorded by Harry W. Paige in August 1965 at St. Francis, South Dakota; translated by the writer.

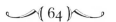

a very special relationship. The ceremony is called the *AlowaNpi*, meaning "to sing for someone," and it has obvious parallels with the Christian ceremony of baptism in which the child obtains new relatives.

Within the wide range of subjects for solo songs are many that deal with intimate matters of the human heart. Songs of love and scorn, despair and death, are included in this rich variety of personal expression. From one point of view these individual songs are the most forceful and direct of all songs. Most of them are spontaneous in contrast to the carefully planned, traditional songs of the ritual or ceremonial. Solo songs also encompass and reflect the activities of what we would call the daily routine. These activities now lack the drama of the buffalo hunt or the warpath, but represent the common, yet significant experiences of which most human life is fashioned. The pre-reservation Sioux probably suffered little from boredom. The daily routine, for them, was the routine of staying alive and staying free, and these are not aims which inspire apathy. The high plains country, which has always inspired, is not the proper setting for tedium. The harsh extremes of nature and climate and their challenges of beauty and destruction produce a poetry of response to life itself. The solo songs of the Sioux share this common denominator with much of modern poetry: any subject is the raw material of song. There is, in fact, among modern poets, a tendency to concentrate on the undramatic, to sing of cabbages rather than kings. A catalog of the subjects of modern poetry would read like a mail-order house catalog. While the modern poet usually proceeds from the particular and common to the universal and uncommon, the primitive does not make the distinction. Most events in his life are important and most things in his environment are important because they serve him or because they are in some way magical; their universal application and significance is well known and needs no couplet to elevate them from the commonplace to the philosophical. The Sioux may sing to the arrow he has made, telling it to fly straight and true. He may sing to a bird, a hoe; to a tooth that aches or a wind that bears a storm. There is, for him, nothing so insignificant that it could not properly be the subject of song.

Individual songs are unique in structure as well as subject matter. Ceremonial participation requires form, but the sudden, often impulsive release of the emotions does not. The opera star may sing as he likes in the shower, but on stage he is performing within a discipline imposed by his art. Ritual is the product of tradition, and because it seeks to achieve some particular end, it is carefully designed. Solo song, even if it does attempt to gain a specific result, is not bound entirely by what has been. It is like the difference between reciting the liturgy in a church ceremony and praying in private. It is the idea that is important, not the form in which it is presented.

For these reasons, solo songs are apt to appear formless and fragmentary, like random thoughts articulated. The divisions of the individual song, where they occur, are inclined to be biological rather than logical. Not only are such songs formless in structure, but they are also frequently obscure in content to all but the singer and the person or power to whom the song is addressed. The following song is a *Wiyoštela OlowaN* or Love Song, that is fairly modern. Most of the older, pre-reservation love songs are concerned with returning from the warpath and, as such, are closely related to the fortunes of war in content. All of the general characteristics of primitive song, considered in Chapter Three, are observed. The Sioux love song is pragmatic rather than romantic: it is designed to summon the lover, not to praise.

wicayaka hecina yau śni	If you are faithful, come!
Wicahpi WakaN	Holy Star
heya helo.[8]	has said this.

Although the moral code of the Sioux was, in most respects, a strict one, it was also one of pragmatic expediency.

[8]John Good. Recorded by Harry W. Paige in July 1964 at Rosebud, South Dakota; translated by the writer.

The accepted courting customs were not elaborate and there was no formal marriage ceremony. In a society in which the males are killed off in war and the children are considered the greatest good and a possible defense against extinction, it would be expected that the rules of courtship, marriage, and even divorce, would be simple and basic. It would be expected that polygamy, though not promiscuity, would be a practical arrangement in a society whose male mortality rate was high. The love songs of the Sioux emphasize the practical rather than the idealistic aspects of mating. This is not to say that romance did not play its part in courtship or that the Sioux did not regard their women with esteem. Winning a mate involved deeds rather than words, and no woman could be interested in a suitor who celebrated her charms in preference to winning a reputation for himself. The color of the lover's hair meant far less than the number of *coups* counted. The purpose of the love song was to make the love known and bring the lovers together. The idea was all important; there was no need for verbal embroidery.

Solo songs are unusually brief, even by primitive standards. The singer knows what he is doing and it is not usually necessary that others share his knowledge. His remarks may be as cryptic and privately symbolic as he wishes to make them. He need not have a sense of audience. In some cases, however, the aim of individual song is communication with others, and in these cases, the songs must be made clear. If the love song or the begging song is not clear, then it fails functionally.

Solo songs frequently employ formula phrases, the cliches of the primitive's expression. The solo song, because it is not ritualistic and ceremonial, does not have to communicate with others. It may be addressed to a god, a spirit, a ghost, or a totem, and, if this is the case, the singer may properly assume that they would know the circumstances of its composition or the nature of the entreaty being made. There is, then, less of an obligation on the singer's part to be explicit. In those cases in which a solo song *is* directed to an audience, e.g., the begging song, formula phrases are still used because they communicate most effectively. The Sioux beggar, singing for coffee and bread, uses the same unadorned language as his modern, city counterpart, who might ask: "You got a dime for a cup of coffee, Mister?" In both cases details are left out in favor of the naked, direct appeal. The failure to elaborate and sketch in the details is also characteristic of Indian graphic and decorative arts.

Once a basic design is decided upon, it is repeated, not presented in realistic detail. In this respect, Sioux painting, carving and beadwork design have qualities known today as "primitive." Because of their brevity and the use of formula phrases, the songs of the Sioux are, by our standards, mere outlines of artistic expressions, but to the Indians they feed the imaginations of the audience. They are the stones dropped in the quiet pool which cause the ripples to spread, even to the shore. In the old times, when a brave warrior was killed in battle, there was no epic composed in his honor. The song of praise might well be limited to several lines, even if he were a great chief. Tribute was not measured by the number of lines or the high poetry of expression, but by the common denominator of grief. Even in more sophisticated traditions, the memorial tribute does not represent an immediate response to sorrow. The poet who first hears of the death of his president may cry: "My God, he is gone!" It is only later, in the solemnity of artistic contemplation, that the tribute begins to emerge as a work of art. The Sioux seldom get beyond the first stage — the immediate reaction. Grief is grief, and should be expressed in all its intensity; but grief recalled in tranquility opens the way to despair in primitive life. In the Indian societies, too many demands are made on the living for them to dwell, Hamlet-like, upon the harsh finality of death. Thus, when a brave warrior named Sitting Crow (KaNġi-iyotake) was killed in an action against the Crow Indians, this song was sung:

kolapi	Friends,
KaNġi-iyotake	Sitting Crow,
kolapi	friends,
kuśni yelo.[9]	returned not.

This song is not even an obituary by our standards. All it tells us is that the warrior, Sitting Crow, is dead. Yet for those who knew him, and perhaps loved him, this bald fact eclipses all others. The song is not designed to convey much information, but rather to solicit and articulate an emotional reaction. It is not necessary to mention Sitting Crow's courage or the number of *coups* he had counted in battle. These things would have been well known to the audience. The song again points out what it is that interests the common conscience — it is the particular fact, unadorned as it may be. There is no attempt to generalize about death and the mysteries of the after life. The singer demonstrates the art of focusing on the significant point, the simple statement that carries the greatest emotional potential. The modern poet might be inclined to look through the eye piece of the telescope and to see the large focus, using the warrior's death as the specific excuse for a general observation or a philosophical leap into the unknown; but the Indian singer looks through the opposite end and uses the instrument perversely, as a microscope.

The reader must also imagine the dramatic performance which undoubtedly accompanied the song. A song of six words — and yet the drama of its singing might have lasted for hours and involved a cast of hundreds. It is not difficult to picture in the mind's eye the dead warrior's mother, her hair loose and flying wildly, her legs and arms slashed and bleeding, her face painted black for sorrow. It is not difficult to visualize the honor march of the warrior society to which the deceased belonged, the members black-faced and chanting the six words solemnly, as though they made up the last sentence of a mighty epic. "Sitting Crow returned not." That is the song. A year from the time of his death, his wife,

[9]Densmore, p. 384.

mother, or child might return to the forsaken burial scaffold that held his remains aloft, there to weep, to sing, or possibly to leave some food as a "spiritual feeding" for the ghost. It may be that his memory demanded an honor song at the annual Sun Dance. These songs, if rendered, would also be as stark and as simple as the one which announced his death.

Brevity and simplicity do not necessarily mean that the song is composed with carelessness or indifference.

tokala kiN	The fox
miye	I am;
taku	something
otehika	difficult
owale yelo.[10]	I seek.

This five-line song may have taken hours, or even days, to compose. From all the relevant aspects of the human condition, the singer must focus on one — the one to which he can respond most fully, and the one that will interest all the other members of the group. His own inspiration may be the starting point, but there is usually a period of gestation and a period of incubation. The singer must find exactly the right words, and although he has formula phrases and a secret shorthand on which to draw, the song must be artistically perfect for him and his fellow tribesmen, or else its power may be lost or turned against them.

In one respect, all the songs of the Sioux are ceremonial, even the solo songs. In the mind of the primitive, almost everything in life that has a significance is worthy of ceremonial attention. The sharpening of an arrowhead, for example, is not without significance in a society of hunters and warriors. There is no need to explain its importance to the group, for its members are well aware of it. An Indian may compose a song as he sharpens the arrowhead, saying that the arrow must be sharp for the kill or the people will go hungry. Having accomplished his task, he may go about the camp, holding the arrow above his head and singing his song.

[10]Densmore, p. 415.

He may dramatize the moment of the kill for all to see. In short, he may construct an artistic ceremony to celebrate his craftsmanship and to win the magical favor of his guardian spirit.

Sioux songs are not separate from the living experiences of the individual. A modern slang expression advises us "not to make a production" of what appears to be insignificant. The Sioux is wont to "make a production" of anything he considers important. To the outsider, it often seems to be a case of "much ado about nothing," the celebration of the inconsequential, from boredom or despair, but it is usually not so. The Indian has his own idea of what is important and what is worthy of artistic production. The singer is an important man among the Sioux. If he is not a warrior, then he is as important as the warrior. It is significant that Sitting Bull, the Hunkpapa war chief and medicine man, wanted to be remembered as a singer as well as a warrior-chieftain.[11]

A secret language is used in individual songs as it is in ceremonial songs. Just as a man's private prayer might appear obscure to another who overhears it, so the solo song of the Sioux is apt to appear cryptic, particularly when the context is not immediately apparent. The songs of healing are, for example, replete with instances of secret language. As the physician of today often employs a jargon that serves to keep his knowledge exclusive, so the Sioux medicine man protects his power and his prestige from those who do not share his spirit or his skill. It is believed that the healer's power is derived in part from phrases in his song, phrases that are expressed in secret language, such as "my heart is different" and "a wind comes to get me." The former is a secret phrase which appears in a number of songs. The second phrase alludes to the north wind that has the power to carry the man who dreams of the wind. The four cardinal points, and the winds which come from these points, are important sources of the power concept of nature for the Sioux.

[11]W. S. Campbell [Stanley Vestal], *Sitting Bull, Champion of the Sioux* (Norman, Oklahoma, 1957), p. 22.

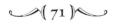

Sometimes, a secret phrase will be expressed by "a wind wears me." This means that the wind has the power to "wear" a man, just as a man may wear an emblem of his guardian spirit around his neck. In some songs, the wind represents an object of dream or vision and is considered the source of power.[12]

Solo songs then, are the Indian's most intense form of expression. He has a song for everything that strikes him with an emotional impact. But it must be remembered that the written word can only *suggest* the beauty of these songs and the performances of which they are a part. The words only *suggest* the sense of security and satisfaction found in them by those who have depended on song for power, prayer and harmony. They are intense emotional experiences re-lived in the drama of artistic creation. There could be no song as direct and as stripped of ornament as the death song, sung by the Sioux as he faced death and the mysterious terror of *wanaġiyata*, the land where the spirits dwell. There are few poets in the records of Western civilization known to have sung their swan song, who have faced death with only the armor of a song. Yet the Sioux has done this — and still continues to do it. The writer will never forget the old woman who lay dying in the alien sterility of a hospital room in Rosebud, South Dakota, in the summer of 1964. She motioned for the nurse to draw open the shades so that she might see the hills, the sun and the sky. Then, in a feeble voice that held no hint of fear, she began to sing her death song. The words were fragile and confused, but the last part was clear:

le makoce waśte	This land is beautiful.
wi kiN	O Sun,
wana	now
ehake	for the last time
waNmayakuwe.[13]	come greet me again.

[12]Densmore, p. 276.

[13]Song by an unknown singer; collected and translated by Harry W. Paige.

CHAPTER FIVE

Ceremonial Songs

IN THE HEART of the Sioux, the ceremonial is not considered as primarily a symbolic representation or the dramatizing of a myth. It is a reality experienced. As such, all Sioux ceremonials have but a single dominant purpose: to seek the aid of the supernatural. The Sioux does not worship *WakaNta-Nka* so much as he appeals to the Great Mystery for aid and power. The Sioux religion is based on this emotional response to *WakaNtaNka*.[1] The Great Mystery is not personified, but represents an all-pervasive, supernatural composite of many of his benevolent gods, including *Wi*, the Sun; *Maka*, the Earth Mother and *Skan*, the Sky. As has been observed in earlier chapters, the Indian mind tends to think in terms of the specific rather than the abstract, and because of this, *WakaNtaNka* becomes manifest in the natural world. Francis Parkman, the first literary man to live with the Sioux, writes of this aspect of their religion as early as 1846:

I knew that though the intellect of an Indian can embrace the idea of an all-wise, all-powerful Spirit, the supreme Ruler of the universe, yet his mind will not always ascend into communion with a being that seems to him so vast, remote, and incomprehensible; and when danger threatens, when his hopes are broken, and trouble overshadows him, he is prone to turn for relief to some inferior agency, less removed from the ordinary scope of

[1]Vernon D. Malan and Clinton J. Jesser, *The Dakota Indian Religion* (Brookings, South Dakota, 1959), p. 8.

his faculties. He has a guardian spirit, on whom he relies for succor and guidance. To him all nature is instinct with mystic influence. Among those mountains not a wild beast was prowling, a bird singing, or a leaf fluttering, that might not tend to direct his destiny, or give warning of what was in store for him; and he watches the world of nature around him as the astrologer watches the stars.[2]

This quotation helps to explain why contact with the supernatural is almost always through dreams or visions which involve animals or other objects found in the natural world. The animals, stones, trees — are to the religion of the Sioux as the revealed scriptures are to the devotees of other religions. Through such things of nature the Indian makes his appeals to the Great Mystery. Though his communication with the Great Mystery is usually a highly mystical, impressionistic experience, it serves him practically to regulate and regularize his behavior in conscious life, and to establish codes of conduct by which he may live. Even the most wildly mystical and subjective of experiences is brought down to earth, influencing, and often directing, practical behavior. Sometimes, however, it becomes impossible for the votary to interpret the experiences that have come to him in dream or vision.

Black Elk, the Oglala mystic and holy man, reveals that he was transported into the other world, the "center of the earth,"[3] and there met the Six Grandfathers who advised him and gave him the power to "make the Nation live." The rest of Black Elk's tragic life was spent in trying to interpret his great vision, to find the practical means by which a dying nation and a people might be saved. The old warrior, who had fought the whites at the Rosebud and elsewhere, finally died in 1950, still searching for the meaning of the vision that had come to him when he was but a boy of nine winters.[4]

[2]Francis Parkman, *The Oregon Trail* (New York, 1962), pp. 201-202.

[3]Black Elk informed John G. Neihardt that the "center of the earth" was Harney Peak in the Black Hills of South Dakota.

[4]Black Elk, *Black Elk Speaks*, p. 63.

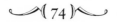

An important by-function of Sioux ceremonials is that they bring the people together in a communal appeal to *Waka-NtaNka*. In pre-reservation days the Sioux split up into small bands for the winter so that they could better survive when game was scarce and ponies had to feed on the bark of the cottonwood. Each band would go to its favorite winter camping ground, usually one protected by high bluffs, one with a good supply of water, wood and buffalo chips. In the spring, the small bands would come together again and celebrate the reunion by rites which also celebrated the fecundity and rebirth of nature. When not engaged in these invocations to the Great Mystery, the people socialized and carried on the business of the whole tribe. The council decided matters of warfare, violations of treaties or hunting grounds rights, and other important business. But most of the people spent their time feasting, singing and dancing, celebrating and visiting. There were other important things to do, however. For now they also conducted the *HuNkapi*, the *HaNblecheyapi* and the Sun Dance rites. Today, the Sioux love these ceremonials as a calling together of the people more than as a spiritual gathering.

Dakota winters are long and severe, and many people have little to do but sit by the wood stove and try to keep warm. Boredom is the ally of cold, hunger and misery. In the spring, the people, like nature, come alive. From isolated parts of the reservation they come, bearing tents, utensils, and precious ceremonial regalia in a pathetic Joad-like caravan. But the people are alive again! Forgotten is their abject poverty and hunger. Forgotten are the hardships and privations of a winter that buried them deeper in isolation and neglect. All their bleak yesterdays seem to be redeemed in this time of celebration and they are as children. The old men step lighter, feeding on the sun and talking themselves into yesterday. They speak of ceremonial things, the men punctuating the silences with their staccato *hau, hecetu* (it is well), and *waśte yelo* (it is good).

Ceremonials also serve to celebrate the mysterious events of the human cycle and to invoke the assistance and protection of the supernatural. The classical scholar, C. M. Bowra, has observed:

The life of primitive man, from birth to burial, resembles a sequence of events in a single ceremonial. At each stage he recognizes that something important is happening and that he must celebrate it in a full and fitting way.[5]

As has been noted in Chapter Four, not all the events of the human cycle are incorporated into established ceremonials involving the whole tribe. For example, no prescribed ritual accompanies the birth of a child, but this does not mean that proper recognition cannot be given to the event, and that it cannot assume the proportions of a ceremony. Great events *demand* recognition: they also demand that a full measure of protection accompany them. As in the Christian ceremonies associated with baptism, confirmation, marriage and death rites, the functions of celebration and the entreaty for divine assistance are combined in the form of ritual. The less man understands of these human events, the more he is inclined to equate them with the mysterious ways of the supernatural, and the greater the necessity for divine intervention. For a people who depend on the bounties of nature for survival, rain, or the lack of it, the migrations of wild animals and the course of growing things are not statistics — they are the means of life. The human and the natural fuse in an ancient interdependency that makes each of their aspects of the greatest possible significance.

Ceremonials are a means of perpetuating the traditional values of the culture. They dramatize those events of the historic past which have helped sustain the people. Among the Sioux, as among most primitive peoples, Tradition is King. The Sioux is, by nature and experience, conservative. *Change,* for him, is usually synonymous with *loss*. Bitter experience has confirmed this fact. In addition, the Indian feels very strongly that both he and his culture are doomed to ex-

[5]Bowra, p. 176.

tinction. His vital need, then, is to pass on old values and traditions; that is why he honors the tribal elders, the grandparents and the "story catchers," who record the myths, legends and songs for posterity. But the greater part of this perpetuation is accomplished through ceremony and ritual. From childhood the full-blooded Sioux is not only exposed to the rituals that dramatize his Indian heritage: he is invited to participate in them. The Sioux, even today, are extremely permissive in rearing their children. To the outsider, it appears that Indian children are all "spoiled" by their parents, especially by their grandparents, who are very influential in educating the young. Discipline seems not to exist, and physical punishment is rare. One old grandmother, who had just spent her last coins on candy for her grandson, explained to an inquisitive white: "Nothing that lives is spoiled by love. The *waściuN* (white man) pets his dog and beats his child. This is *witko* (crazy). It is always better to love."[6]

In pre-reservation days, the games of Sioux children were imitations of the serious ventures of hunting and warfare. The *HuNkapi*, described in detail later in this chapter, is a ceremony for the benefit of the child. There was even a child's version of the solemn Sun Dance, which took place after the main ceremony, and included an imitation of the torture rites by piercing the skin with cactus spines.[7] Sioux children once grew up steeped in the traditional lore of the people, and were familiar with all of the dramatic ceremonials which engaged their elders. There is still a great amount of public approval which accompanies the participation of children in public rituals, not only for the children themselves, but for their relatives.

In a culture without written literature, the ceremony becomes the living drama by which the old ways are perpetuated: they are a renewal of tradition and cultural heritage. Old culture heroes and their deeds are kept alive. In most

[6]Remarks overheard by the writer at the trading post in St. Francis, South Dakota.
[7]Densmore, p. 137.

INITI OR PURIFICATION LODGE

—*Harry W. Paige Photo.*

of the important ceremonies, honor songs remind the people of the greatness of their Nation and its leaders, men who "walked the red road," and kept the old ways in their hearts. If these rites encourage the Sioux to look backward, they also help him to face the future in a technological and alien society. They give the contemporary Sioux a sense of stability, a sense of unity, and a sense of reverence. They tell him who he is.

Most Sioux ceremonials represent a concentration of ritualized power by *WakaNtaNka's* elect. It is characteristic of the thought of primitive peoples to consider themselves as the original, chosen people and to consider all others as outsiders. The word *Kiowa*, for example, means "we are the people." The Cheyennes refer to themselves as *Tsis-Tsis-Tas*, the True People.[8] The Sioux, also, regard themselves as the Real People. In their genesis myth, they disclaim relationship with any other people on earth. A great flood is said to have descended on the Plains at a time when the world was young. All nations were destroyed by the deluge and most human life was magically transformed into red pipestone. A great eagle swooped down from the sky and permitted a beautiful maiden to grasp its talons. Then the eagle carried her to the safety of a high cliff above the torrent. When the water subsided, the woman gave birth to twins, fathered by the war eagle. This is the mythological account of the beginning of the Sioux Nation.[9] Because they are the Real People, it is believed that the Great Mystery will harken to them, individually and collectively. Theoretically, there is power in numbers, even in the realm of the spiritual. The Christian also believes that through a concerted effort his prayers may influence the divine will to assert itself in the affairs of man — to take pity on him, or to help him through some terrible crisis. Sioux ceremonials, then, are concerted entreaties to the Great Mystery, more powerful because they represent an intense, harmonious articulation by *WakaNtaNka's* elect.

[8]Grinnell, p. 4.

[9]*Legends of the Mighty Sioux* (Sioux Falls, South Dakota, 1960), pp. 45-46.

The ritual dramatizes the relationship between man and the supernatural. Even the circle *(gmigmela)* in which the people camp is arranged so that the tipi entrances face the rising sun. The circle is geometrically symbolic of the people's origin in, and final return to, *WakaNtaNka,* in the never-ending cycle of birth and death. The circle is also symbolic of the unity of the people. Preparatory rites are often miniature dramas in themselves, designed to purify the body and spirit of the votary so that he may be in a state pleasing to the Great Mystery. Sage, smoke, water, isolation, fasting — all these are employed to prepare the body, while prayer, supplication, dream and vision are used in the preparation of the spirit. These preparatory rites are often elaborate and painful, as in the case of the prolonged fast or the staring at the sun. The Sioux believe pain subordinates the flesh, and its self-infliction dramatizes man's dependence on the supernatural. One of the familiar cries in the Sioux ceremonial is: *"UNśimala ye! UNśimala ye!"* (Pity me! Pity me!) On the battlefield, or boasting in his "kill talks" of the *coup* he had counted, the Sioux was often proud and arrogant, but in the spiritual presence of the Great Mystery, he tends to be humble and contrite, for he feels that without the intervention of the supernatural he is powerless and his people are without a center.

Ceremonials have distinguishing characteristics. They are designed for specific purposes, all of which are concerned with the appeal for power. These purposes are not essentially different from those of individual songs, but they are infinitely more complex, and they involve the welfare of all the people. In their complexity, they combine the artistic elements of music, song, dance, prayer, and symbolic action. In contrast to solo songs, they are highly ritualistic, and no deviation from tradition is usually tolerated. These ceremonies have usually been dictated by tradition; most have been "given" to the Sioux by a supernatural being, considered to be the agent of the Great Mystery. Therefore, the time and manner of conducting them are carefully prescribed. Because ceremonials are ritualistic and therefore pageant-like, they call for the active participation of the whole group. They may last for days, or even weeks, and most other aspects of Sioux life are suspended during this time to permit a complete concentration on the spiritual.

The wide range of Sioux ceremonial life is illustrated by their seven sacred rites: the *Inipi* or the Purification Rite; the *HaNblecheyapi* or the Vision-seeking Quest; the *AlowaNpi* or the Singing Over Someone: the *Waki Caġapi* or the Keeping of the Soul; the *Iśna Ta Awi Ca LowaN* or the Preparing a Maiden for Womanhood; the *Tapa WaNka Yap* or the Throwing of the Ball, and the *Wiwanyank Wacipi* or the Sun Dance (literally, "Looking at the sun they dance"). Two of these rites, the *Inipi* and the *HaNblecheyapi*, have subsequently been revised to incorporate elements believed to have been introduced by the mythical White Buffalo Maiden. Because they are often used as preparation for major ceremonies they have a special importance.

Inipi is the shortened form of *Inikagapi*, meaning "they revitalize themselves."[10] It is the rite performed by the Sioux to purify the body and spirit for communication with the Great Mystery. Before any important undertaking, the Sioux enacted the *Inipi* rite to be certain of his purity. Black Elk says that his tribesmen performed this Purification Rite daily, or even several times a day in pre-reservation times, and he equates the neglect of this ritual with the loss of power suffered by the Sioux since following the white man's road.[11] Yet this rite is still conducted by the traditional Sioux. By some Indian homes on the reservation today stand small shelters made of bent willow branches and covered with animal skins, canvas or cloth. These are *Initi;* in them now, as in the past, the Sioux purifies himself, using all the Powers (Elements) of the world — earth, air, fire and water. He

[10]Stephen E. Feraca, *Wakinyan: Contemporary Teton Dakota Religion* (Browning, Montana, 1963), p. 27.

[11]Black Elk as told through Joseph Epes Brown. *The Sacred Pipe* (Norman. Oklahoma, 1953). p. 43.

heats rocks, representing Mother Earth, in a sacred fireplace called *Peta-OwihaNkeśni*, Fire of No End.[12] He pours water over hot rocks to make steam, the primary agent of purification. He uses sage and sweetgrass to rub on his body. Cleansed of impurities of body and spirit through the *Inipi*, the votary can now see through *CaNte Iśta*, or the Eye of the Heart, which permits him to see all that is true and good. Today, most of the songs in the *Inipi* ceremony consist of vocables, although the word *TuNkaśila* (paternal Grandfather) is heard frequently in these vocables. In former times, as today, sacred chants were offered as the devotee went through the elaborate steps of the ritual:

WakaNtaNka, we give thanks for the Light which you have given us through the Power of the place where the sun comes up. Help us, O You Power of the East! Be merciful to us![13]

The *HaNblecheyapi* or "Crying for a Vision," discussed briefly in Chapter Two, is like the *Inipi* in that it was sacred to the Sioux as one of their oldest ceremonies. Black Elk, one of the best informants about sacred things, refers to this rite as being "at the center of our religion."[14] Both men and women were once encouraged to seek a vision, not only for the power they received, but for the strength of all the people. The importance of receiving a vision cannot be overemphasized. Without it, a man was nothing, for he was not aware of the source of his power. All of the great leaders of the Sioux attributed their power to a vision they had received, usually as a result of the *HaNblecheyapi* rite.

Most of the formalized aspects of the rite are conducted through a holy man, who acts as a spiritual advisor to the "lamenter." The rites may be conducted to learn the source of one's power, to petition *WakaNtaNka's* aid in curing the sick, or to give thanks for favors already granted. Perhaps

[12]*Ibid.*, p. 42.
[13]*Ibid.*, p. 43.
[14]*Ibid.*, p. 44.

the most common reason for "crying for a vision" is to attain a mystical spiritual unity with the Great Mystery. On the advice of a holy man, the votary purifies himself by the *Inipi* rite and begins his lonely vigil, often on a distant butte or mountain top, for from one to four days, if necessary. During the vision-seeking quest the lamenter abstains from food and drink. In pre-reservation days he might even mutilate himself by cutting off a finger or by otherwise mortifying the flesh. He usually stares at the sun and faces the four directions for long periods of time, crying:

WakaNtaNka	O Great Spirit
uNśimala ye	be merciful to me
oyate wani wachin cha.[15]	that my people may live.

The lamenter watches carefully for what appears to be a sign from *WakaNtaNka* — the roll of thunder, the flash of lightning or the cry of an animal. Whether or not the lamenter receives his vision depends on both his character and the success of his preparations. Usually, after several days of fasting, torture, and loneliness, he is rewarded. If he is not, it is assumed that he is not yet spiritually prepared for communion with the Great Mystery. As a part of his vision, the Sioux may also receive songs, to be sung when there is a need for power. The following is a song received in a vision by Charging Thunder. An old wolf appeared to him and informed him of how to make a sacred pipe that would prevent the enemy from detecting his approach. The old wolf directed him to sing this song whenever he used the pipe:

wakaNyaN	In a sacred manner
mica kelo	he made for me
caNoNpa waN tokeca	a pipe that is different.
wakaNyaN	In a sacred manner
mica kelo	he made for me.
naġi ksapa waN	A wise spirit
maka hewaye	I met
wakaNyaN	in a sacred manner.

[15]Black Elk, *The Sacred Pipe*, p. 57.

⌒⌐⟨ 83 ⟩⊢⌐⌐

mica kelo	He made it for me.
kola	Friend,
waNmayaNka.[16]	behold me!

After receiving his vision, the lamenter returns to camp and has the holy man interpret it for him. From that time on, he identifies with the object of his vision: he actually *becomes* the essence of the animal or thing revealed to him. As tangible evidence of his success in spiritual communion, he carries some appropriate talisman — the wing of a hawk, a sacred stone, or the claw of a bear. It becomes the most important thing in his life, the source of his power and, more importantly, a source of strength for his people.

The sacred pipe (*PtehiNcala CanoNpa*) is considered the most *wakaN* possession of the Sioux, and the office of the "Keeper" of the sacred pipe is a solemn responsibility. These "keepers" traditionally live to very old age, most of them to about one hundred years.[17] According to one recent informant, the sacred pipe is now kept at the Cheyenne River Reservation in northwestern South Dakota.[18] A number of the "old timers" have made pilgrimages to see what they believe to be the sacred relic, symbol of the very life of the Sioux people, for it is said that without the pipe the people will perish.

The accounts of the coming of the White Buffalo Maiden are substantially the same, although there is no general agreement as to the time of her coming. An extract from the Winter Count of High Hawk purporting to show the significant event of the year corresponding to 1540 represents a primitive sketch of her coming.[19] The Sioux usually say that

[16]Densmore, p. 183.

[17]Densmore, p. 66.

[18]Wilbur A. Riegert of Wounded Knee, South Dakota. This location of the sacred pipe has been confirmed more recently in a correspondence from Stephen E. Feraca, who says that the pipe is in the keeping of a thirteen-year-old boy "keeper" on the Cheyenne River Reservation.

[19]Oliver LaFarge, *A Pictorial History of the American Indian* (New York, 1956), p. 164.

it was "many winters ago" or "at a time when the earth was young." One mid-summer, when the Tetons were gathering together, as was their custom, two scouts were appointed to go in search of buffalo. When they had separated and met again, they saw a solitary object approaching from the west. As it came nearer, they saw that it was a beautiful maiden, dressed in white buckskin. The Maiden addressed them saying that she had been sent on a sacred mission by the Buffalo Tribe. She told the scouts to return to their people and inform the chief to erect a special lodge facing the direction "where the sun rolls off the earth." She also told them that the lodge should be located in the middle of the camp circle. They were to spread sage at the place of honor and to prepare a small square altar for the buffalo skull and other ceremonial objects. The White Buffalo Maiden informed the scouts that she had an important message for the people and that she would appear in their camp at sunrise. As she was telling them these things, one of the young men had bad thoughts. A cloud came down and settled over him. When it lifted, only his bones were left, and they were covered with snakes. The Maiden told the other young man to return to his camp — without looking back. He did as she requested and returned safely to camp, where he informed the chiefs and tribal elders of what had happened. Preparations were begun at once to comply with the Maiden's directions, and the people received word of her coming with great joy. Early the next morning, all the people gathered around the special lodge and waited. Exactly at sunrise, the Maiden entered the camp, singing this song:

niya taNiNyaN	With visible breath
mawani ye	I am walking.
oyate le	This nation
imawani	I walk toward,
na	and
hotaNiNyaN	my voice is heard.
mawani ye	I am walking
niya taNiNyaN	with visible breath;

mawani ye	I am walking.
waluta le	This sacred relic
imawani ye.[20]	[for it] I am walking.

Escorted to the place of honor, the White Buffalo Maiden informed the people that they should regard her as a sister. She praised them, saying that the people were known for their reverence for sacred things. Then she presented them with the sacred pipe, symbol of the covenant between the Buffalo Tribe and the Sioux. She also told them that the pipe was to be used as an instrument of peace between nations and as part of the magical rites in ministering to the sick. She addressed, in turn, the women of the tribe, the children, the men, and finally, the chief. She told them that *WakaNtaNka* was their Grandfather and that they must hold fast to sacred things and "walk the red road." "By this pipe the tribe shall live," she is reported to have said. She offered the pipe to *WakaNtaNka*, pointing the stem to the sky, the earth, and the cardinal points. She then outlined the moral and ethical codes which would be celebrated in their ceremonials. As soon as she left the camp circle she magically turned into a white buffalo (*ptesaN*), a creature still regarded as sacred by the Sioux. The coming of the White Buffalo Maiden may be considered as the mythical genesis of the Sioux Nation. She figures prominently in most of their ceremonials, at least by allusion and metaphor.[21]

The *HuNkapi* or The Making of Relatives, was believed to have been promised the Sioux by the White Buffalo Maiden and is one of the most beautiful of their ceremonials. According to Black Elk, it was *Lakota Matohokšila* (Bear Boy), a holy man, who received this rite in a vision.[22] This represents one of the mythical interpretations of the rite. Modern scholarship now believes that "... the ceremony may have dif-

[20]Densmore, p. 68. The *mawani* in lines 2, 7 and 9 should be *wamani* and *imawani* in lines 4 and 11 should be *owamani*.

[21]Densmore, pp. 63-66.

[22]Black Elk, *The Sacred Pipe*, p. 101.

fused from the Poncas and is relatively recent."[23] The rite is symbolic of man's relationship with the Great Mystery: as *WakaNtaNka* loves his children so man must demonstrate a love for one another. It also serves as the ceremonial binding of two children. The ceremony is sometimes known as *AlowaNpi*, which means "to sing for one," the *HuNka* being the child who is "sung over." The rite is also thought to be symbolic of the relationship between the White Buffalo Maiden and her adopted children.

The greatest blessing among the Sioux is that of a child, and in the *AlowaNpi* rite a man who performs the ceremony is regarded as a father of the child for whom it is sung or, in the case of the binding of two children, the two are considered as brothers or sisters. Both are considered the most binding tie that can be established, for it is made freely. The essential object used in this ceremony is a decorated wand called the *HuNka CanoNpa*, which represents the pipe given to the Sioux by the White Buffalo Maiden. The wand is decorated with the head and feathers of a woodpecker, a simple and responsible bird in caring for its young. The *AlowaNpi* ceremony may be sung for more than one child at a time and it frequently represents the fulfillment of a vow made at some time of crisis. The parents of the child for whom the ceremony is planned send an invitation, symbolically represented by the pipe, to the second father or the child being bound ceremonially to theirs. If the individual so honored accepts the invitation and the responsibility that goes with it, he opens the case in which the pipe is wrapped; if he sees fit to decline, he returns the case unopened. Once acceptance is made, elaborate preparations begin.

The ceremonial lodge is built. An altar is prepared in the lodge, and fresh sage is strewn upon it to receive the painted buffalo skull whose horns are decorated with strips of red cloth. In back of the buffalo skull a pipe rack is set to hold the ceremonial pipe. Also, an ear of corn on a stick painted blue (symbolic of the heavens) is placed near the pipe rack.

[23]Stephen E. Feraca, in a correspondence to the writer, March 19, 1967.

As the culture of the Tetons is not an agricultural one, considerable speculation has arisen as to the purpose and history of the ear of corn used in the ceremony. Although the Sioux, in the Woodlands, practiced some agriculture, this ceremony probably derives from one of the Village tribes, probably the Ponca. The ceremonial use of the corn sticks also was probably borrowed from the Poncas or Omahas.[24] High Eagle, an informant of Frances Densmore's, explains the ceremonial use of corn by telling the story of an old couple who had never been blessed with children. They had appealed many times to *WakaNtaNka*, usually during the Purification Rite. One day, as they were performing this rite, a voice told them that the next day their wish would be granted. The next morning, in front of the old couple's lodge, they saw a plant which had started to grow. The mysterious voice told them to care for the plant and observe its development and it would grow into a beautiful child. Soon the plant grew to be tall and beautiful and, as soon as it started to turn in color, they removed the corn from the plant. From this mysterious experience the old couple concluded that this was the child sent by *WakaNtaNka* for them to care for and raise as their own.[25]

The *ItaNcaN* or Leader begins the ceremony by getting the child for whom it is to be performed. He pretends not to know where the *HuNka* (the child being honored) lives, and wanders about the camp singing:

HuNkapi	The HuNkapi, [those being honored]
eca	I wonder
tukte	where
tipi so.[26]	they live.

When the *ItaNcaN* finally arrives at the child's lodge, he relates the important deeds of the family for all to hear. Then he gets the child or children and together they go to the

---

[24]Stephen E. Feraca, in the correspondence cited in the previous footnote.
[25]Densmore, p. 73.
[26]*Ibid.* The *eca* in 1.2 might be better translated as "over there."

ceremonial lodge. There, the six-rendition *HuNka* song is sung to the accompaniment of a rattle.

le huNka	This honored one,
eca	behold,
waNkaNtu kiN	you who are above.
le huNka	This honored one,
eca	behold,
maka ciN	you who are in the earth.
le huNka	This honored one,
eca	behold,
wiyohpetata	you who dwells where the sun falls.
	(West)
le huNka	This honored one,
eca	behold,
waziyata	you who dwell in the home of the giant.
	(North)
le huNka	This honored one,
eca	behold,
wiyohiyaNpata	you who dwells where the sun returns.
	(East)
le huNka	This honored one,
eca	behold,
itokagata.[27]	you who dwell in the direction we face with outstretched arms. (South)

As in practically all Sioux ceremonies, the *ItaNcaN* invokes the spirits of Earth, Sky, and the four cardinal points. Collectively, these encourage the presence of *WakaNtaNka*. The *HuNka* honored by the *AlowaNpi* receives many spiritual benefits by this demonstration of affection, and it is believed that he will have nothing but good in life. The child or children may keep the ceremonial pipe and wand as reminders of the love shown in the ceremony. Also, it was the custom to present other gifts to the honored ones. The year 1801 is known in one Winter Count as *Awica AlowaNpi*

[27]Densmore, p. 75.

Waniyetu or Truthfully Singing Winter, an allusion to the year of the first *AlowaNpi* ceremony.[28]

Traditional Sioux still honor their children in the modern equivalent of this old way, referring to the contemporary rite as the Beloved Child Ceremony. The writer attended one of these ceremonies on the Rosebud Reservation and observed that the old *HuNka* Song is still used, although it had been reduced to four repetitions each of the first two renditions. The spiritual aspects of the ceremony had been de-emphasized in favor of the social: there was much singing and dancing, feasting and giving presents to the honored child. The atmosphere was very much like that of the birthday party. One old grandfather, who had presented the *HuNka* with two horses, went about singing:

le huNka	This honored one,
le huNka	this honored one,
śuNkawakaN	horses
wecuNwe.[29]	I donated.

An old lady, dressed in white buckskins and her ceremonial regalia, chanted the single word *HuNka* over and over as she handed out ice cream sticks to the waiting children.

Waki Caġapi or the ceremony of Spirit Keeping, is intended, like the *AlowaNpi*, to show love — in this case for a deceased loved one, usually a child. By performing this rite, the Sioux believe that the spiritual drama will also increase the love for one another among the living. The "keepers" of the spirit gain both spiritual and temporal benefits from the performance, and this is another example of the combined spirituality and pragmatism of the Sioux, and of their harmony of religious expression. The *Waki Caġapi* prolongs the mourning period by "keeping the spirit"

[28]Densmore, p. 69. The reader's attention is called to the fact that the Winter Count date, 1801, appears to contradict the ancient origin of the rite as related in the gift-of-the-pipe myth.

[29]Sung by the grandfather of Gloria No Heart of Rosebud, South Dakota in August 1965; translated by Andrew No Heart. Later, the donation proved to be the *cash equivalent* of two horses.

of the deceased for months, or even a year, and then ceremonially "releasing the spirit." During the period of "keeping," the mourner cannot share in the military, political or social life of the tribe or band. He is expected to isolate himself from worldly concerns and concentrate on the ceremonial expression of his grief. The White Buffalo Maiden is said to have given this ceremony to the Sioux and it is appropriate that the principal song rendered is the one allegedly sung by the Maiden when she first appeared to the tribe.[30] As the Keeper of the Spirit *(Wanaği Yuhapi)* served as the ceremonial leader and principal singer, he was free to compose his own songs, chants and prayers. Except for the Song of the Maiden, then, the songs of this ceremony do not remain constant; therefore, a brief summary of the rite will suffice.

The Keepers of the Spirit, after proper purification rites have been conducted, cut a lock of hair from the deceased and this, together with some of the possessions of the dead, comprised a "spirit bundle," kept in a special place of honor in the Keeper's lodge. A "spirit post," carved from a cottonwood, was painted to resemble the deceased, and this was placed outside the Keeper's lodge. After a definite period of mourning, the spirit was released, and all involved in the rite expressed their thanks to *WakaNtaNka* that the spirit was now reunited with its spiritual source of being.

The *Waki Cağapi* has fallen into neglect since the Sioux moved on to reservations and came under the influence of Christianity. The missionaries attempted to suppress the rite, branding it as "heathen": they encourage the substitution of memorial services and Masses for the "pagan" practice of spirit keeping. The result, as has usually been the case, has been a fusing of the old and new into a hybrid ceremony featuring *both* native and Christian elements: the "spirit post" and the Mass card continued for a while to remind the Sioux of their beloved dead.

There is no puberty rite as such for Sioux boys. The *HaNblecheyapi*, described earlier in this chapter, appears to serve

[30]Densmore, p. 68.

this purpose, equating the "Crying for a Vision" with the traditional manhood rites of most primitive societies. Sioux maidens do have a ceremony which marks their initiation into womanhood and symbolizes their future roles as wives and mothers. The rite is called *Isna Ta Awi Ca LowaN*, which means literally "Her Alone They Sing Over." The ceremony is performed after the first menstrual period, and its purpose is not only to recognize the physical changes which accompany this time, but also to instruct the young woman in the things she will need to know in assuming her new role in the tribal society. Black Elk recalls that before this ceremony had been given to the Sioux, a young woman was isolated in a special tipi during her menstrual periods.[31] This period is considered a source of potential danger to the Sioux, a time when the powers of the holy man may be taken from him by this defilement. Even today, the traditional Sioux are particularly apprehensive about menstrual activity at times of illness, religious ceremonials or at times when other magical rites are conducted.

Black Elk reports that Slow Buffalo gave this rite to the people after having seen a vision of a buffalo cow cleaning her new born calf.[32] On the strength of this vision, Slow Buffalo became a holy man and created a ceremony to make the people holy through their women who, at this *wakaN* time seemed like Mother Earth, the symbol of fecundity. Several moons after his vision, Slow Buffalo performed this rite for a girl of fourteen winters called White Buffalo Cow Woman Appears. As in the *HuNkapi* ceremony, the people construct a ceremonial lodge and gather together the necessary ceremonial objects: a buffalo skull, water, sweetgrass, sage, some cherries, a sacred pipe and some red and blue paint. The following day, after everything is ready, Slow Buffalo seats himself at the west side of the sacred tipi and prays, holding sweetgrass over a bed of live coals in front of him. The smoke ascends to *WakaNtaNka* in the form of a visible prayer. Then

[31]Black Elk, *The Sacred Pipe*, p. 116.
[32]*Ibid.*, p. 117.

the holy man places the sweetgrass on the coals, purifying the pipe, the skull and other ceremonial objects. He prays again, this time specifically for the young woman to be purified, invoking the power of the four directions, the earth and sky. Because of his prayers the sacred tipi becomes symbolically a microcosm'of the universe, the rite transcending the particular and pretending to universal significance. The holy man fills the pipe and smokes, offering the sacred object to the earth, sky and the four cardinal points. He prays for the maiden to be purified, but he also prays for the generations to come, invoking the special intercession of Mother Earth, the symbol of fertility:

O Mother Earth, who gives forth fruit, and who is as a Mother to generations, this young Virgin who is here today will be purified and made sacred; may she be like You, and may her children and her children's children walk the sacred path in a holy manner.[33]

The holy man then points the stem of the pipe towards the buffalo skull, acknowledging by his prayer that the rite being performed is in imitation of the buffalo cow who cleans its young. Thus, he makes an identification with the "four-leggeds" as well as with the powers of the universe. The maiden, after having been purified by the *Inipi* rite, is escorted into the sacred tipi by her closest relatives, the only ones allowed to witness these sacred rites. As these people watch, the holy man purifies himself in the smoke of the sweetgrass. Then he sings the song that the buffalo taught him in his vision:

> Le waNyak a-upe!
> WakaN okaspe waN kicanwain kta ca.
> HeoN waNyak a-u we.
> Tatonkaska WiN el
> Cekiya yaNka wakaN ca.
> Eyuha waNyak a-upe.[34]

[33]Black Elk, *The Sacred Pipe*, p. 117.

[34]*Ibid.*, p. 122. Translated into Lakota from the English text by James E. Emery of Rapid City, South Dakota.

SUN DANCER DRAGGING BUFFALO SKULL

—*Harry W. Paige Photo.*

> This they are coming to see!
> I am going to make a place which is sacred.
> That they are coming to see.
> White Buffalo Cow Woman Appears
> Is sitting in a *wakaN* manner.
> They are all coming to see her.

After this rendition, the witnesses seem to feel that his power truly comes from the closest of all "four-leggeds," the buffalo, and also from the strength of his vision. As he finishes his song, he roars, imitating the bellow of a buffalo. A red dust comes from his mouth ". . . just as a buffalo cow is able to do when she has a calf."[35] The holy man blows the red dust over the young virgin six times. Then he scoops out a hollow of loose earth and, taking a pinch of tobacco as an offering, presents it to the sky and places it in the center of the hole. Using loose tobacco, he scatters it to form a line from east to west, and another from north to south. This tobacco cross insures that the powers of the universe are now gathered together in this microcosm, this sanctified place. On top of the tobacco cross he draws a line of blue paint. Black Elk interprets the profound significance of this painting as follows:

> The use of this blue paint is very important and very sacred, if you understand the meaning, for, as I have often said, the power of a thing or an act is in the understanding of its meaning. Blue is the color of the heavens, and by placing the blue upon the tobacco, which represents the earth, we have united heaven and earth, and all has been made one.[36]

The holy man places the buffalo skull on the mound of earth, its face pointing east. Then he paints the skull with red stripes and, placing sage into the empty eye sockets, then sets a bowl of water before the skull. He places a few cherries in the water, for they represent the fruit of the earth. Next, he makes a bundle of sweetgrass, the bark of the cherry tree and hair from a live buffalo. As the maiden holds this bundle

[35] Black Elk, *The Sacred Pipe.* p. 123.
[36] *Ibid.*

over her head, the holy man explains that she now has become like the tree of life, a symbol of fertility and promise. The maiden sits down on the earthen floor and the holy man relates in detail the secret of his power, gained through his vision. After he finishes, he sings another holy song:

> Lena oyate kiN wakaN pe;
> Makosintomniya wawaNyaka-u we.
> Tatonkaska WiN Cekiya waNke heoN;
> Eyuha wawaNyak a-upe.[37]
>
> These people are sacred;
> From all over the world they
> are coming to see it.
> White Buffalo Cow Woman Appears
> is sitting here in a *wakaN* manner;
> They are all coming to see her.

Imitating the actions of the buffalo, the holy man pushes gently with the buffalo skull until the young woman is standing before the bowl of water. She kneels and takes four sips, one for each of the cardinal points. When she rises, the holy man places a piece of buffalo meat in her mouth. Then the buffalo meat and the bowl of water are passed around, each one partaking of the food and drink. This act of communion marks the close of the ceremony. Then the celebrants feast and hold a "give away," in which food and horses are given to the poor of the village. It is possible that this rite, perhaps initiated within the memory of Black Elk, who died in 1950, has some elements that might be considered Christian. The taking of the meat and drink could be considered a form of Holy Communion. The tobacco cross might have Christian symbolic value, although the cross was used as a symbol long before Christianity. It is also just as possible that the *Iśna Ta Awi Ca LowaN* is a native rite, perhaps instituted by Slow Buffalo, perhaps revived by him after a long period of neglect.

---

[37]Black Elk, *The Sacred Pipe*, p. 125. Translated into Lakota from the English text by James E. Emery of Rapid City, South Dakota.

Certainly the rite has a dual purpose as revealed in its songs: the purification of a young woman and the invocation of power for the people. As in all Teton religious ceremonies, the sacred tipi becomes an image of the universe. There is a universality about the events enacted there. The people are coming to see the ceremony "from all over the world." All the people are to share in this symbolic rite. What is ostensibly the recognition of physical changes in a maiden is a prayer as well — an appeal for the well being af all the "two-leggeds" and "four-leggeds" of the earth. To accept an Indian ceremonial at its face value alone would be to misrepresent its real meaning for the native.

The *Tapa Wanka Yap* or "The Throwing of the Ball," is the last of the seven sacred rites reported to be given to the Sioux by the White Buffalo Maiden. Black Elk says that *Waskn-mani* (Moves Walking) received this rite in a vision given him by the Maiden "many winters ago."[38] The rite is in the form of a game, but it has great spiritual significance. After receiving instructions from the holy man, the people erect a sacred tipi on the perimeter of the camping circle and cover the floor of the lodge with sage. Just before the Sun comes up, the holy man walks about the camp announcing that this day is holy because the White Buffalo Maiden will be with them again. Hearing this news, the people follow him about the camp and accompany him to the sacred tipi. The holy man enters the tipi and sits facing the east while his helpers bring coals from a fire. He then places sweetgrass over the coals and, as the smoke rises, prays to WakaNtaNka. When the sun rises, he takes an axe and, after presenting it to the earth, sky and the four cardinal points, strikes the ground at the four quarters. Using the axe and a knife, both of which have been purified in smoke, the holy man fashions an altar made of earth. With a pointed stick he draws a line from east to west and another from north to south. He places tobacco in these small furrows and paints it red to represent the earth. The altar now becomes the universe in miniature

[38]Black Elk, *The Sacred Pipe*, p. 128.

and the Great Mystery lends his real presence to the sacredness of the rite.[39] While one of the helpers beats a drum, the holy man sings the song of the sacred pipe, *CaNnumpa WakaN OlowaN:*

Kola lecuN ye! Kola lecuN ye! Kola lecuN ye!
Lecel ecanhaNtas hetuNkaśila waniyankiN kte.
WakaN ocokaN el nayajiN na
Canupa caNli oyaglala cana miksuya yo,
Lecel ecanu haNtas wayala kiN yuecetu kte.

Kola lecuN ye! Kola lecuN ye! Kola lecuN ye!
TohaNl wakaN kagapi el nayaji cana-
WakaNtaNka ho eyayakiya cana
NituNkaśila waniyankiN kte.
NaNku wayala hena yuecetu kte.

Kola lecuN ye! Kola lecuN ye! Kola lecuN ye!
Ecanu kinhan nituNkaśila waniyaNkin kte.
TohaNl ceya estamni ojuya ho eyayakiya cana-
Wainuge hena niceyuecetu kte.

Kola lecuN ye! Kola lecuN ye! Kola lecuN ye!
NituNkaśila cangleska wakaN el
WaNkatakiya yugulnayaji wanyanke kihan-
Nita woawacin eyuha neciyuecetu kte.[40]

Friend do this! Friend do this! Friend do this!
If you do this your Grandfather will see you.
When you stand within the holy circle,
Think of me when you place the sacred tobacco
in the pipe.
If you do this He will give you all that you ask for.

Friend do this! Friend do this! Friend do this!
If you do this your Grandfather will see you.
When you stand within the holy circle
Send your voice to *WakaNtaNka.*
If you do this He will give you all that you desire.

[39]Black Elk, *The Sacred Pipe,* p. 130.

Friend do this! Friend do this! Friend do this!
If you do this your Grandfather will see you.
When you stand within the holy circle
Crying and with tears send your voice to *WakaNtaNka*.
If you do this you will have all that you desire.

Friend do this! Friend do this! Friend do this!
That your Grandfather may see you.
When you stand within the sacred hoop
Raise your hand to *WakaNtaNka*.
Do this and He will give you all that you desire.

The song is regarded as very powerful, for it was given to the
people by the White Buffalo Maiden at the time she brought
the sacred pipe. As the drumming dies, a young girl is led
into the tipi by her father and after walking around the inside
of the sacred lodge following the course of the sun, she sits
to the left of the holy man. Taking a ball made from buffalo
hair covered with hide, he paints it red, the color of the earth.
At the four quarters he paints blue dots, representing the
heavens. After the painting, the ball is considered sacred, the
symbol of the union of the heavens and earth. The ball is
then purified in tobacco smoke. The holy man then presents
the ball to the girl who holds it in her left hand, raising her
right hand to the heavens. As she remains in this attitude, the
holy man prays. The girl represents the generations to come
and she stands before *WakaNtaNka*, holding the universe in
her hands. When he finishes the prayer, he goes to the altar
and paints the buffalo skull with red lines. Then he relates his
vision, describing a white buffalo calf magically transformed
into a young girl. In his vision the girl threw a ball to each of
the four directions and the buffalo, now transformed into
human beings, scrambled to catch it and return it to her. Her
last throw was straight up and, as the ball came down again,
she and the people were once again transformed into buffalo.

After revealing his vision, the holy man explains the symbolism of the game they are about to play. The ball is the uni-

[40]*Ibid.*, p. 131. Translated into Lakota from the English text by James E.
Emery of Rapid City, South Dakota.

verse and also *WakaNtaNka*, whose home is the universe. All the people must try to catch the ball and whoever does so will receive a great blessing for himself and for the people. The holy man leads the girl from the sacred lodge to an open place suitable for the game. The girl stands in the center of the ring of people and throws the ball toward the west. The person who catches the ball returns it to her. She repeats this action, throwing the ball toward the other three directions. Finally, she throws the ball straight up and the people rush to catch it. Black Elk summarizes the symbolic significance of the rite:

. . . Just as *WakaNtaNka* is eternally youthful and pure, so is this little one who has just come from *WakaNtaNka*, pure and without any darkness. Just as the ball is thrown from the center to the four quarters, so *WakaNtaNka* is at every direction and is everywhere in the world; and as the ball descends upon the people, so does His power, which is only received by a very few people. . .[41]

The ceremony is extinct today, and only a few of the older people remember it at all. One can imagine Black Elk, nearly blind and close to the spirit land, listening to the squeals of the Sioux children playing ball in the school yard near his home at Manderson, South Dakota. Surely he must have thrown his mind back to a happier time — to a time when he too struggled to catch a ball, not to score a point or win the applause of the crowd, but so that the people might live. In 1947, a few years before his death, he made the forlorn prophecy of one who has outlived his time:

At this sad time today among our people, we are scrambling for the ball, and some are not even trying to catch it, which makes me cry when I think of it. But soon I know it will be caught, for the end is rapidly approaching, and then it will be returned to the center, and our people will be with it. It is my prayer that this be so.[42]

The *Wiwanyank Wacipi* or "Looking at the Sun They Dance," is perhaps the most significant and enduring of all

[41] Black Elk, *The Sacred Pipe*, p. 137.
[42] *Ibid.*, p. 138.

Teton ceremonials. It is the only surviving ritual which involves the whole tribe. According to Black Elk, a Sioux named *Kablaya* (Spread) received instructions for this rite in a vision. This, Black Elk says, took place ". . . many winters after our people received the sacred pipe from the White Buffalo Cow Woman."[43] Most contemporary Indian opinion about the origin of the Sun Dance is derived from such respected leaders as Dewey Beard, William Gay and Tom American Horse, all recently deceased. Some students of the culture of the Plains Indian feel that the Sun Dance is an adaptation of the medicine lodge ceremonies of the Cheyenne and Arapaho.[44]

None of Miss Densmore's informants in 1911 could tell the history of the ceremony. One of her informants, Red Bird (*Zitkala Luta*) says that ". . . there came a year when the sun died. There was a period of darkness, and from that day a new religion came to the Indians."[45] Miss Densmore feels that Red Bird refers to the eclipse of 1869, and that the "new religion" is apparently Christianity. Although some scholars have pointed out the parallels between the Sun Dance ceremony and Christian practices, it would seem highly unlikely that the rite was Christian in origin.[46] Such parallels include the similarity between the cross and the Sun Dance pole with its choke-cherry bundle that resembles a cross in place; the blood sacrifice of Christ and that of the Sun Dancers; the crown of thorns and the crown of sage worn by the dancers, and the suffering of Christ for man and the suffering of the dancers for the welfare of the People. The best evidence indicates that the Sun Dance has native origins and came to the Sioux during the period of its diffusion on the Plains:

The various forms of Sun Dance quite obviously have a common origin, for certain basic elements are common to them all. It is

[43]Black Elk, *The Sacred Pipe*, p. 67.
[44]Feraca, *Wakinyan*, p. 11.
[45]Densmore, p. 86.
[46]Feraca, *Wakinyan*, p. 15.

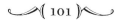

evidently a combination of many widely differing features, some of which disappeared as it spread, others of which were added. Since there are some eighty different features in all, fourteen of which may be described as basic, there can be an infinite number of variations in the dance as performed.[47]

Whatever its origin, the Sun Dance is the most typical of all Plains Indian ceremonialism. It contains all the aspects that would appeal to a warrior-hunter society. The elements of endurance, sacrifice and trial by torture are all consistent with their social and religious concepts. Such a rite is designed to test the four great virtues of the Tetons: generosity, courage, integrity and goodness. It tests these virtues by appealing to the power of the sun. Of all the manifestations of *WakaNtaNka, Wi* or the Sun is believed to be the most powerful, and it has always occupied a prominent place in the myth and ritual of the Plains Indians. The Sun Dance was the only tribal gathering for a religious celebration and it took place in early summer, when the sun had warmed the earth, usually in the Moon of Fattening (June) or the Moon of Cherries Blackening (July), at a time when the ceremonial sage was in bloom, the moon was full and the people were prosperous and happy.

Talk of the Sun Dance is considered "sacred talk" by the more traditional Sioux and even today some of these older Indians speak of it with reverence. Officially banned by the government in 1881, there are still a few old timers who bear the scars of *sub rosa* dances held in remote sections of the reservations from time to time. In most cases, the votary performs the rites in thanksgiving for special favors received from *WakaNtaNka*. One of the writer's informants, who wished to remain anonymous lest the spiritual effects of the dance be nullified by revealing "sacred talk," danced in fulfillment of a vow he had made when his child was critically ill. He promised *WakaNtaNka* that, if his child recovered, he would offer his flesh in gratitude. When the child did recover,

[47]Kaj Birket-Smith, *Primitive Man and His Ways* (Cleveland, 1960), p. 93. This interpretation is also supported by Stephen E. Feraca in *Wakinyan,* p. 11, by Leslie Spier and others.

despite the physicians' dark prognosis, the father went through his ordeal as he had vowed.

In pre-reservation days the vow was usually made in gratitude for favors received on the warpath or the buffalo hunt. Spiritual benefits for the whole tribe were insured by participation in the ceremony, and a man might offer his flesh "so that the people might live," as did Sun Dancer Lorenzo Eagle Road, on June 20, 1965. The Sioux believe that a man's body is all that he really owns in this life, and it therefore becomes a fitting sacrifice to the Great Mystery. The Sioux may give food to the poor or tobacco offerings to the cardinal directions, but the offering of one's flesh is considered to be the greatest of all gifts.

Another important purpose of the ceremony, common to many tribes of the Plains, is to replace the diminishing energy of the universe.[48] The cosmology of the Plains Indian is, in general, limited to the world: the sun, moon and stars are important, but only insofar as they are considered as extensions of this earth. The Siouan concept of the "universe" is quite limited, especially by modern scientific standards. The Sioux, even in their mythology, are not very interested in *who* created the earth and *why*. They are more interested in the existential fact that the world *is*. They see the world system as a mechanistic one: the energy of the universe is running down like a great battery according to a regular schedule of cyclic change. The Sioux believe that the energy of the universe runs down because men do not live as they should: they do not adapt their behavior to the orderly plan revealed in nature, but try to dominate and control nature. This leads to disorder — natural, ethical and moral. In the Western tradition we find this cyclic view expressed poetically by William Butler Yeats in "The Second Coming":

> . . . The darkness drops again; but now
> I know
> That twenty centuries of stony sleep
> Were vexed to nightmare by a rocking cradle,

[48] E. Adamson Hoebel, *The Cheyennes: Indians of the Great Plains* (New York, 1966), p. 84.

And what rough beast, its hour come
round at last,
Slouches toward Bethlehem to be born?

The Sioux also use the beast image in their mythology, but it
is the image of the buffalo rather than ". . . a shape with lion
body and the head of a man" as Yeats envisioned. According
to one of their myths, at the beginning of this present cycle a
buffalo was placed at the west in order to prevent a great deluge which threatens the earth. Every year this buffalo loses
one of its hairs and every age it loses one of its legs. When the
buffalo is completely without hair and legs the water will
flood the earth and a new cycle will begin.[19] Such a view may
probably be traced back to the observation of a corresponding cyclic pattern in nature, e.g., the changing seasons, the
phases of the moon and the human cycle. Given this cycle
and their mechanistic view, the Sioux believe that the main
assistance the people can receive from the supernatural is
ritual knowledge of the world, that is, how it operates and
what to do to renew the earth. *WakaNtaNka,* and his manifestations in the spirit world, know these things.

Knowledge yields power and power insures the continuation, even the prosperity, of all life. Thus, the native power
concept is dependent on knowledge. The greater purpose of
the Sun Dance then is to restore the dissipating energy of the
universe; to recharge the battery; to place the cosmic urges
toward creation and order into some kind of equilibrium
with the opposing forces of destruction and disorder. Basic-
ally, this is the world view of the primitive and it is astonish-
ing to note that it is very similar to the view of modern
physics. The most widely-accepted theory concerning the
dissipation of energy states that the entropy or energy of the
universe *unavailable* for work is increasing. To put it another way, the energy *available* for work is running down, a
fact which increases the probability of disorder. In modern
physics, ultimate disorder is not conceived as a deluge that
will rush in over the bones of a buffalo, but as a "heat death"

[19]Black Elk, *The Sacred Pipe,* p. 9.

or fiery explosion of the universe.[50] Though the metaphor has changed, the end result remains the same and in both cases is expressed in poetic language.

At present, the physicist has no theories of how to halt this disorder or how to reverse the process of dissipation. The Sioux Indian did: he knew what to do so that the people might live. He had been "told" by *WakaNtaNka* through the White Buffalo Maiden and other spiritual agents. He must renew the energy of the universe through ritualistic regeneration if crops, animals and men are to survive. Man can never *control* this energy: he can only attempt to replace it by his ritualistic behavior which must be, in turn, consistent with his faith and moral conduct.

The proper ritual of the Sun Dance developed in the old days went as follows:

Although the place of the Sun Dance changes from year to year, the whole tribe knows where to go. The smaller bands make their way to the great tribal reunion after wintering in their favorite spots. They usually arrive at the sacred place several months before the ceremony is to take place in order to make the necessary preparations. They raise their tipis in the great circular encampment, each band in its own special place. Then the people construct the *initi* or sweat lodges used in the rites of purification. Spiritual preparations are going on all the time, dating from the time when vows are declared, whether privately to *WakaNtaNka*, or publicly. After settling at the Sun Dance grounds, the tribal leaders, including those of the powerful warrior societies, meet in council to conduct the business of the tribe. Later, criers (*eyapaha*) go about the camp announcing the instructions for the ceremony. The whole encampment is like a giant ant hill of activity: the atmosphere is charged with expectation, hope and general good will. The people shed the happy tears of reunion. Children and dogs are underfoot in noisy confusion. A mother whose warrior-son has been res-

[50]Dr. Martin Martin, Department of Physics, Clarkson College of Technology, Potsdam, New York, in a conversation with the writer in December 1966.

OMAHA DANCERS AT THE OGLALA SIOUX SUN DANCE

—Harry W. Paige Photo.

cued from the Crows, pierces the day with her cries of thanksgiving. For her, the Sun Dance time is ripe with new promise. The young man's father hurries about the camp declaring his vow to give one hundred pieces of his flesh. The people understand. *Waśte yelo! Le pejuta waśte!* It is good! This is good medicine!

A month before the ceremony a medicine man (*Waka-NhaN*) prays for fair weather — dancing, smoking and singing to insure the proper conditions. He sings a song handed down from the holy man, Dreamer-of-the-Sun:

> aNpetu wi taNyaN hinapa nuNwe
> maka ozaNzaNyaN taNyaN
> hinapa nuNwe
>
> haNhepi wi taNyaN hinapa nuNwe
> maka ozaNzaNyaN taNyaN
> hinapa nuNwe.[51]
>
> May the sun rise well.
> May the earth appear
> brightly shone upon.
>
> May the moon rise well.
> May the earth appear
> brightly shone upon.

After the weather rites are conducted, the warrior societies meet with the tribal elders and leaders to organize the Sun Dance. These warrior groups — the Strong Heart Society, the White Horse Riders, the Fox Society — are made up of men of great prestige among the Sioux. These warriors now name the four young men who will have the honor of selecting the Cottonwood tree to be used as the sacred Sun Dance pole (*CaNwakaN*) and the four young virgins who will fell the tree. They also elect an older man of spotless reputation who is well versed in traditional lore and ceremonial decorum to act as Intercessor (*Kuwa Kiyapi*). The Intercessor

[51]Densmore, p. 100.

is by tradition a holy man or medicine man: he usually retains the office of Intercessor as long as he continues to be venerated by the people. His duties include the offering of prayers for the people, preparing the sacred place, singing the ceremonial songs and painting the sacred tree. The Intercessor accepts the honor in a spirit of deep humility. "*Miš-nala wimacaśa yelo*," he says. "I am only a man." The people are pleased by his remark; they know he will do his best at this holy time. The tribal council also chooses the man who will be the Leader of the Dancers. He, like the Intercessor, must be a man of established reputation. His duties are to provide the sacred buffalo skull and the sacred pipe and, of course, to lead the dancing. These two officials represent all the people in petitioning *WakaNtaNka*: they must themselves be men spiritually endowed with blessings from the Great Mystery. This means that they have received a vision and have had frequent communication with *WakaNtaNka* or one of His manifestations.

Other preparations for the ceremony include the making of tobacco offerings, tied in small packets to painted sticks. The women and old people do this while sitting in the shade, working their fingers deftly as darning needles. The Leader of the Dancers rehearses the singers and dancers, making certain that each song is perfect, each movement of the dance contributes to the total spiritual effect desired. At this time the young men and women selected to take part may be challenged by any member of the tribe. *Wicahpi* (Star), one of the maidens chosen to assist in cutting down the sacred tree, is challenged. She has had a brief flirtation with one of the warriors in the Strong Heart Society. She did nothing wrong, but there is some suspicion and there should be none at this sacred time. *MakapejutawiN*, Earth-medicine Woman, is chosen to replace her. This right to challenge and express the "will of the people" helps to insure that only the most worthy are chosen. The period immediately before the ceremony, with only the last minute preparations to be made, is devoted to socializing and celebrating Sioux heroes in song and dance. It is at this point that the people sing their honor song to the memory of *KaNġi-iyotake* (Sitting Crow). Many people weep openly, remembering the lonely burial scaffold on the prairie. This is also the time that porcupine quill bead-work (*wakśupi*) is made and cherished ceremonial costumes are taken from their deerhide cases and made like new. Feathers, like the men who wear them, grow old and bent. There are persistent rumors that the sacred pipe, given to the tribe by the White Buffalo Maiden, has been brought from the Powder River country in the north to insure the special blessings of this Sun Dance.

On the morning before the day of the ceremony, the four young men go in search of the sacred tree to be used as the Sun Dance pole. The Cottonwood selected must be straight and slender, as nearly perfect as possible. The young men sing their individual war songs as they search for the tree, for it is now considered as an enemy to be overcome. When the young men select a tree, they return to the camp in triumph, as they might have returned from a victorious war party. The people greet their arrival with singing, dancing and feasting. Then a large party leaves to cut the tree and carry it to the place where it will be raised. Many go to wit-ness the cutting of the holy tree, some to make offerings when the tree finally falls. The children follow the crowd quietly, sensing the solemnity of the occasion. The Inter-cessor leads the group, followed by the four young men who selected the tree and the four virgins who are to cut it down. After them comes the Leader of the Dancers, carrying a purified axe that has never been used before. After arriving at the site, the Intercessor prays and presents the sacred pipe to the earth, the sky and the four directions. The people be-lieve that *WakaNtaNka* is now present and a blanket of silence falls over the great crowd.

One of the four virgins is selected to cut the tree. Before she strikes a blow one of her kinsmen is allowed to relate one of his great deeds. His name is *Mato WaNbli* (Eagle Bear) and he tells how he rescued a fallen comrade in an engagement with the Pawnee. The people greet his heroic tale with a chorus of approval: *Hau! Hecetu! Waśte Yelo!* The virgin raises the axe and makes a feint at the tree. Then she passes the axe to the other three virgins and they do the same. After each pass at the tree, a kinsman of each maiden relates an account of his bravery. The axe then returns to the first maiden; this time she cuts until the thirty-five foot tree falls to the south. As it strikes the ground, the Intercessor and the singers lift their voices in song:

itesabye	The black face-paint
owale	I seek;
ca hecamoN	therefore I have done this.
śuNkake	Horses
owale	I seek;
ca hecamoN.[52]	therefore I have done this.

The felling of the sacred tree is like a victory over an enemy: the *itesabye* is the black face paint the warrior puts on when he has conquered a foe. The medicine men burn sweetgrass as the branches are stripped. One branch is left, about a quarter of the distance to the top, so they may tie the chokecherry shoot nest to it. From this time on the tree is considered *wakaN*. No one may step over it. The people still remember the young woman who became angry when she was not selected as one of the maidens to cut the tree. Her heart was bad and she stepped over the sacred tree to show her anger. When she returned to camp, a pony kicked her in the head and she died that same day. The heart must be good at this time; jealousy and anger must be thrown away. Thirty men carry the tree, walking by twos, the top of the tree to the front. The tree must not touch the ground. The party stops to rest four times as the tree is set on V-shaped limbs carried for that purpose. As the tree is carried into the Sun Dance circle the people surge forward, crying their prayer offerings to the tree. Young men strip away the bark and the Intercessor paints the tree with vermilion stripes. The crowd becomes quiet as he sings:

[52]Densmore, pp. 113-114.

ate	Father,
lena tawa makiye	all these he has made me own:
caN makobaza	the trees and the forests
najin	standing
hiyeye cin.[53]	in their places.

As the Intercessor finishes his song, the six-foot nest is tied in place with leather thongs. Two rawhide effigies, one of an Indian, the other of a buffalo, are attached to the bar. There are eight of these thongs, a pair for each of the four brave ones who will offer their flesh. A tanned buffalo hide is tied on the top of the pole and, after first packing the hole with buffalo tallow, the pole is set in the opening and slowly raised by many willing hands. A great cheer bursts from the people as the pole drops into place, the crossbar pointing north and south. When the sound subsides, the Intercessor begins to sing:

wakaNyaN	Sacred
nawajiN ye	I stand.
waNyayaNka yo	"Behold me,"
emakiye con.[54]	was said to me.

The people have placed the pole so that it is in the exact "center of the earth," that is, in the Sun Dance circle, about fifty feet in diameter. A few feet west of the pole the people prepare an altar called *OwaNka WakaN* or "The Sacred Place." Then they erect a pine-covered shelter around the circumference of the area so that the spectators, the relatives of the dancers and the old people may be protected from the burning sun.

On the morning of the Sun Dance the people rise early and watch the eastern place where the sun will rise. One old man mutters a half-prayer, half-prophecy: *"Le aNpetu waśte."* This day is good. The people watch as a golden stain fills the east, the prelude to *WakaNtaNka's* age-old ritual. A mighty cheer swells as the sun is born again this holy day. The medicine man who had prayed for fair weather smiles

[53]Densmore, p. 117.
[54]*Ibid.*, p. 119.

SUN DANCE POLE

inwardly: his power is still strong. He has not known a woman these three months, saving his strength for this single prayer. Now, *WakaNtaNka* has rewarded him. It is good.

The four who are to be suspended from the pole and those who will give pieces of flesh, begin their march to the *Initi,* the purification lodges. They have not eaten for a day and have taken little water. They have prayed much during the night, begging the Great Mystery to accept their sacrifice and to have pity on the people. The younger children gaze at these heroes as they pass, their small, black eyes holding wonder like a cup. Truly, these men who will endure the agony of the thongs are the greatest among the Sioux. It is a holy kind of courage that they will show. A few minutes after they enter the *Initi,* the children hear a song that seems to rise on clouds of escaping steam:

ho	A voice
u wayin kte	I will send:
namahon ye	hear me
maka	the land
sitomniyaN	all over.
ho	A voice
ye wayelo	I am sending.
namahon ye	Hear me;
wani ktelo.[55]	I will live.

After the dancers go through the purification rites, they are painted by men assigned to this duty by the Intercessor. The man painting each dancer chooses a color that is associated with one of his dreams of the sky: blue, yellow, white or black. Blue is symbolic of the cloudless sky; yellow represents the forked lightning; white is the light; and black symbolizes the darkness. One of the dancers has a dark blue line across his forehead; another has the red circle of the sun painted on his chest. The dancers wear their hair loose, in the manner of warriors who have killed an enemy. The dancers are bare-footed, and each wears a deerskin apron. The Intercessor goes

[55]Densmore, p. 124.

to each one and places an eagle-bone whistle around his neck. After the painting and dressing, the dancers retire to the dance lodge of their own band until they are summoned by the crier.

The Intercessor and the Leader of the Dancers wait in the large council tipi. The Intercessor wears red paint on his face and hands and his buffalo hide vest is trimmed with human hair, symbolic of enemies slain. The crier goes about the camp announcing: "*Wana u po! Wana yustanpe. Ihaḫni po!*" Now all come! Now it is finished! Hurry ! The sacred time is here. The solemn procession begins. The Intercessor is the first to enter the Sun Dance circle, bearing the sacred pipe with the stem upraised. The Leader of the Dancers walks a few paces to the rear, carrying the buffalo skull, now painted with red stripes. A friend or relative of the Leader of the Dancers carries his pipe, which will be placed by the buffalo skull. The men who have made vows walk on either side of the Intercessor and the Leader of the Dancers. On the outside of the group come the war societies, marching in ceremonial dignity. The pageant-like procession stops at the entrance of the Sun Dance circle. The Intercessor raises the stem of his pipe to the east and each of the men to be tested that day offers a silent prayer to that direction. It is a simple prayer: *WakaNtaNka, uNśimala ye!* Great Mystery, pity me! The procession passes the southern point of the circle and proceeds to the western point, where the Leader of the Dancers lays the buffalo skull on an altar bed of sage, the skull's sage-filled sockets seeming to stare vacantly at the blazing east. He then places the pipe on its wooden rack, stem pointing to the east, but often to the skull or west. The Intercessor burns sweetgrass in his pipe, letting the smoke rise toward the heavens like wisps of prayer. Then he draws on the pipe, offering the stem to earth, sky and the cardinal points. The Leader of the Dancers repeats his actions and so do all of the individual dancers. The men who are to fulfill their vows go to the Sun Dance pole and face it so that they are looking eastward, into the sun.

The Leader of the Dancers shouts: "Repent! Repent!" A great answering cry of sorrow comes from the people. As soon as the sound dies, the large drum, south of the Sun Dance pole, is struck. This is the signal for the men to begin dancing with arms upraised in supplication and faces turned to the sun. The singers, both men and women, are seated around the drum, the women sitting behind the men. The Intercessor rises from his seat, west of the "sacred place". When the wordless dancing song is over, he sings the opening prayer:

tuNkaśila	Grandfather,
ho uwayiN kte	a voice I am going to send —
namaḣon ye	hear me
maka sitomniyaN	all over the universe.
ho uwayiN kte	A voice I am going to send.
namaḣon ye	Hear me,
tuNkaśila	Grandfather:
wani ktelo	I will live.
epelo.[56]	I have said it.

The first man to fulfill his vow dances close to the sacred pole and lies down, his eyes still following the path of the sun. The medicine man kneels over him and, lifting the flesh of his breast, thrusts a bone awl through it. The votary's lips, cracked with thirst, tighten as the awl plunges beneath flesh and muscle. The medicine man places a stick between the dancer's jaws so that he may bite down on it. The pain is easier to bear with something in the mouth. The flesh is pierced over each breast and a blue stick is thrust through the bleeding wound. The medicine man helps the dancer to his feet and ties the thongs to the two sticks: the other ends of the thongs are already fastened to the cross-bar of the Sun Dance pole. As the man begins to dance — toe, heel; toe, heel — rising to the toes and then back down — his wife begins a high, keening cry to tell him that he is brave and that her heart is with him in his suffering. Then she dances from the crowd into the circle and stands behind him, doing the

[56]Densmore, p. 131.

woman's dance — bending from the knees and then back up in time with the drum beat. The man does not seem to notice her: he is staring at the sun, blowing shrill blasts on the eagle-bone whistle in his mouth. He dances backward several steps, passing the weight of his body against the thongs. His flesh is drawn out like a woman's breasts and the blood flows freely. Sweat runs into his eyes and the sun sears like a living flame.

Another dancer has promised to carry eight buffalo skulls suspended from his flesh. Each of the skulls weighs twenty-five pounds. The medicine man pierces his flesh so that he can carry four in front and four in back. Painfully, he begins to circle the pole, always on the worn perimeter of the circle. His face is turned to the sun. He too blows on his whistle as he dances to the strict beat of the drum — toe, heel; toe, heel. He will not be free of his holy burdens until the sun rises the next morning.

The father of the one rescued from the Crows steps forward. He has vowed to give one hundred pieces of flesh in spite of his white hair and the weight of many winters. Cries of approval go up as he steps forward to show his thanks that his son is alive. The medicine man thrusts the pointed awl into his breast and digs out a piece of flesh the size of a small berry. The old man winces but he does not cry out. Tears of pride come to his wife's eyes: the old warrior is still brave and he has much thanks to give. The medicine man lifts the piece of flesh to the sky. It is not an official part of the ceremony, but he declares in a loud voice: "This brave man has promised to give his flesh. Now he makes good his promise." Some of the people weep to see the old man's pain, but they are tears more of pride than sorrow. After the twenty-second piece of flesh is removed, the old man faints and lies limp and bleeding in the dust at the foot of the pole. The people are silenced by his fall, wondering what will happen. Suddenly, the sound of the drum is drowned by a great cheer and a hundred keening cries. The old man's son steps forward, not looking at his father's twisted body. The young man is still weak from his period of captivity and he limps from a wound, but he moves to the pole and awaits the medicine man's thrust. Before the awl can strike, ten young warriors of the White Horse Riders step forward to take his place. The people cheer wildly: "It is good to be a Lakota!" they cry.

All morning the ordeal continues. The dancer carrying the buffalo skulls has pulled away from three of them. They lie behind him in the dust as he dances away — like the bloody births of his agony. Two of the dancers faint. One struggles to his feet in a wild triumph. He has seen a vision of a white eagle carrying four arrows in its talons. He stumbles as he dances, driven by his vision, blowing harder on his whistle. He falls again, but his strength now comes from the eagle of his vision. He rises again, searching for the sun through nearly blinded eyes.

One man falls and does not rise. He cannot go on. His relatives give four horses to the poor and he is released from his vow. The people are respectful: they know that flesh is weak and sometimes fails. The man is carried into the shade by tender hands, and water is forced to his parched lips. One of the dancers in the circle is crying aloud, but his words are lost in his thirst and pain. His wife, standing behind him, raises her voice to sing for him:

waNbli-iyali	Climbing Eagle (man's name)
heye le	said this:
WakaNtaNka	"WakaNtaNka
uNśimala ye yo	pity me
letaNhaN	from henceforth;
tehaN wanikktelo	for a long time I will live."
eyiN nahaN	He is saying this, and
tehiya najin ye.[57]	stands there, enduring.

Another cry goes up from the people. It is a good thing for a woman to sing for her man in this way.

Now, the sun is directly overhead. The drums are silent and the people stand in hushed attention. The Intercessor steps to the center of the sacred circle and places his palms on the pole as he sings the Noon Song:

[57]Densmore, p. 135.

SUN DANCERS. OGLALA SIOUX SUN DANCE

—*Harry W. Paige Photo.*

tokiya	Where
wakaN	holy
waNlake	you behold
wi cinape ta	in the place where the sun rises;
wakaN	holy
waNlaka nunwe.[58]	may you behold.

The man who has received the vision of the white eagle begins to sing, his breath coming in painful gasps:

WakaNtaNka	WakaNtaNka
ca wakiya caNna	when I pray to him,
namahon e	heard me.
taku waśte	Whatever is good
maku welo.[59]	He grants me.

Shadows lengthen and the sun rolls off the earth, but the dancing continues. All night the dancing will go on. There are brief intervals of rest now, but no food or water. The whistle cries are weaker, but there is some relief: the burning sun has gone down.

When the sun rises the next morning, the Intercessor sings his greeting in behalf of the people:

le miye yelo	Here am I.
waNmayaNkiye yo	Behold me!
anpe wi kiN miye yelo	I am the sun.
waNmayaNka yo.[60]	Behold me.

The people gaze at the sun. They are tired, and feel the pain of the dancers. But there are promises to keep. The drum sounds, reminding them that the ordeal of faith and endurance is not finished. It is a difficult thing — this giving thanks to *WakaNtaNka*. Yet there is much to be thankful for: the people live, and the sacred hoop binding them together is stronger now. The Sun Dance continues.

For the Plains Indians, and for the Sioux in particular, the Sun Dance has traditionally been the ceremonial expression

[58] Densmore, p. 138.
[59] *Ibid.*, p. 140.
[60] *Ibid.*, p. 149.

of their relationship with the Great Mystery and the only public testimony of their spiritual beliefs. Red Bird, one of Frances Densmore's informants, characterized the Sun Dance as ".... our first and only religion."[61] Black Elk has said that the purpose of the Sun Dance is to "... purify the people and to give them power and endurance."[62] History seems to confirm the importance of the rite for the Tetons: the last Sun Dance with torture rites was held in 1883. From this time until the late 1920s the Tetons held no Sun Dances.[63] Yet despite this long period of neglect, the Indians revived the rite with great enthusiasm. Non-Indian reaction to the Sun Dance, especially to the torture rites, has been just as enthusiastic in its denunciation of the ceremony. V. T. McGillycuddy, agent for the Oglala at Pine Ridge, wrote in his report for 1882: "The heathenish annual ceremony termed 'the Sun Dance' will, I trust... be soon a thing of the past."[64] James G. Wright, agent at the Rosebud Reservation, described the Sun Dance as an "... aboriginal and barbarous festival."[65] The Christian missionaries, the officials and employees of the Indian Bureau, the military and the white press echoed an angry chorus of protest against this native "barbarism."

The contemporary Sun Dance of the Sioux represents many things to many people. Some regard it as a perversion of a noble and spiritual rite. At Pine Ridge in 1965, of the four-day ceremony only one hour was devoted to the piercing ritual, although three hours of five mornings were devoted to other parts of the ceremony. For much of the time the people "dance Omaha," or engage in Indian dancing that is primarily social.

Concessions to the tourist are apparent everywhere; both the 1964 and 1965 Oglala Sioux Sun Dance ceremonies did

[61]Densmore, p. 86.
[62]Black Elk, *Black Elk Speaks*, p. 96.
[63]Feraca, *Wakinyan*, p. 11.
[64]V. T. McGillycuddy, quoted in Densmore, p. 86.
[65]James G. Wright, quoted in Densmore, p. 86.

not begin until nine o'clock in the morning although traditionally, the dancers are expected to begin with the rising of the sun. The piercing of the dancers' flesh is not deep: the wounds sustained are superficial. The average time for the dancers to pull away from the Sun Dance pole is about twenty minutes. Many no longer take the rules for pre-ceremonial fasting seriously, and spiritual preparations for the sacrifice are reduced to a minimum. Breaches of ceremonial decorum are very much in evidence. A Sun Dancer will sometimes be seen drinking the white man's *kapopop* (soda) shortly before the ceremony. Some people regard the Sun Dance as a carnival, completely devoid of spiritual significance. Others consider it little more than a tourist attraction. Some believe the ceremony to be *wakaN*, a diluted, but still powerful dramatization of their faith. It is impossible to invest the contemporary Sun Dance with a single meaning. The writer has witnessed three of these ceremonies and it is his opinion that the Sun Dance *does* fill certain basic and vital needs of the Indian people — needs that may be considered under three general headings: cultural, social and spiritual.

It has already been suggested that the Indians feel that their traditional values and patterns of living are being absorbed in the complex of white American life. This fear is, of course, not unfounded. Culturally, if not physically, the Indian is indeed the "vanishing American." He still faces extermination as an Indian and this fate is no less painful when it is accomplished by absorption rather than bullets. The white man has not only taken the Indian's land, his source of food, his gods; he has taken away his reasons for living. The older, more traditional Indian might well agree with Albert Camus' Caligula when he complains:

To lose one's life is a little thing, and I will have the courage when necessary. But to see the sense of this life dissipated, to see our reason for existence disappear: that is what is unsupportable.

Everywhere the old culture is being destroyed, directly or indirectly, by the whites and the complexities of modern life.[66] The older Indian now clings to the last vestiges of his traditional culture. Most of the young follow the white man's road. The middle aged stand at the crossroads, not knowing which way to turn. This cultural demise is perhaps the Indian's greatest fear. The prophetic words of Black Elk find their echo in many an old Indian's heart:

... you see me now a pitiful old man who has done nothing, for the nation's hoop is broken and scattered. There is no center any longer, and the sacred tree is dead.[67]

Today, the traditional Sioux tends to consider the Sun Dance an important link with the past. He sees it as affording an opportunity to exult in what remains of his cultural heritage. He is, of course, aware that the public Sun Dance is a watered-down affair, made weak by time and the white man's disapproval. In the course of the ceremony he sees old ritualistic ways observed carelessly or completely neglected. He tends to accept these concessions with a stoic resignation. He seems to feel that a careless Sun Dance is better than no Sun Dance. In the course of the Sun Dance celebration he still has his moments of pride: when the arena is filled with as many as three hundred and fifty stomping, costumed dancers; when he sees his grandson dancing in the old, Indian way, or when the high falsetto of a competent singer rises to honor one of the great men among the Sioux. In such moments he may assume an alien identity, and then the cheap souvenir trailers, the festooned soft drink and hot dog stands are obscured in a deeper moment of remembrance.

Socially, the Sun Dance celebration fills a vital need of the Sioux for overcoming the boredom of reservation life and for renewing kinship ties, so essential to their social and moral

[66]The Pan-Indian movement, popular with all age groups, is an expression of a new identity for the American Indian and his traditional institutions. As such, it represents a counter-force to the destruction of traditions and native identity.

[67]Black Elk, *Black Elk Speaks*, p. 276.

lives. Families are re-united, old friends meet, grandparents indulge their grandchildren, young people court and make new friends — all in an atmosphere of relaxed conviviality. Tents are set up according to kinship and community groups, and there is a new spirit among a tired people. They see themselves as the center of attraction: white tourists snap their pictures, students question them about parts of the ceremony, governors and senators put in a quick, hand-shaking appearance, a local Olympic hero is honored in song, and for a short time it seems as though the Sioux have redeemed centuries of neglect with this brief moment of recognition. For a people who have lived for nearly a century neglected and apart from the main current of American life, it is almost impossible to convey the effects of this new sense of dignity and importance that the ceremony inspires. The writer recalls overhearing a tourist ask an older Indian about the purpose of the ceremony he was witnessing. The Indian replied simply: "It allows us to endure the other three hundred and sixty-one days of the year."

As most of the Sioux today consider themselves Christians, their worship appears to exclude ceremonies like the Sun Dance. Even the relatively modern nativistic movements like the Native American Church (Peyote Cult) are essentially Christian, though there are strong native elements in their rituals. There is a strong tendency among Indians to see no conflict in combining older, native elements with Christian doctrine and practice. The two well-established Christian sects (Roman Catholic and Episcopalian), on both Pine Ridge and Rosebud Reservations, have met with greater success among Indians not only because they were there first historically, but because they have often been tolerant of Indian traditions, values and patterns of thinking.

The intelligent clergy has recently taken the realistic attitude that the old beliefs should be incorporated within the framework of Christianity rather than suppressed. Churches and their furnishings are frequently built and designed to appeal to the Indian imagination. Our Lady of the Sioux, a

ALTAR AT OUR LADY OF THE SIOUX CHAPEL
OGLALA, SOUTH DAKOTA

—Photo by Father Steinmetz, S.J., Holy Rosary Mission.

Catholic chapel in Oglala, South Dakota, on the Pine Ridge Reservation, is a dramatic example of an attempt to bridge the aesthetic and spiritual gap between the traditional and the new. The altar cloth is a buffalo hide with the words *wakaN, wakaN, wakaN* lettered on it. The carved wood figure hanging on the cross above the altar represents an Indian, rather than a white Christ. The candles are held in buffalo horns. Thunderbirds, lightning, and sacred pipes design the walls. Just as there are differences in church design, there are also liturgical differences in the service itself. The Indian may be a Christian, but he is also an Indian. Success in religion, in human relationships, or in agency politics all depend on the recognition of this simple fact.

The Sun Dance, though it has connections with Christianity, seems to fill a vital need of the Sioux and other tribes of the Plains. No ceremonial is more typical of the spiritual drama of the Sioux. The rite incorporates the high mysticism, the blood sacrifice, and the public humiliation and entreaty which are so significant in the religious beliefs of the Sioux. Christian ritual may satisfy many of the spiritual needs of the Sioux, but the Sun Dance is the living link with a past that is considered by some as being greater than the present.

The Sioux consider the obligation imposed by a dream fully as binding as that required by a vow. Earlier paragraphs have considered the Sun Dance as the fulfillment of a vow made to *WakaNtaNka* by individual members of the tribe. So significant is the vow that if none was made, the Sun Dance would not be held. The Sioux regard the dream as a source of inspiration and spiritual power. They believe that the nature of the dream corresponds to the character of the one who receives it. Thus, a weak man would not have dreams of spiritual strength like those of a chief or medicine man. A dream usually includes directions as to how to conduct one's life. It may also contain songs and reveal a totem. The man who receives a dream is obliged to make it public as soon as possible. By doing so, he allies himself with others who have had a similar dream. In this way the Elk Dreamers are joined together in a secret society whose members recognize the Elk as the source of their power. Those who dream of the wolf or the buffalo are likewise united by their common dreams, considered to be *wakaN*. The various dream societies have rules for conduct in war and peace, as well as special ceremonies for strengthening their power. There are many such societies among the Sioux, but the most powerful is the one which unites those who have dreamed of the sacred bird, *WakiNyaN*, the Thunderbird. Such an individual is called a *Heyoka* or Fool, and the ceremony which announces and strengthens his power is the *Heyoka Kaga* or Fool Impersonation Ceremony.

The traditions and literature of Western Civilization also recognize the paradox of the Fool. From Don Quixote to Dostoevsky's Prince Myshkin, the Fool has traditionally been regarded as having a power of his own; he is to be suspected for this power as well as ridiculed for his actions. Don Quixote's "madness" is the power of the poetry of imagination to overcome a harsh and often brutal reality. The Fool and the wise man; the Fool and the Innocent; the Fool and the Saint — are frequently one and the same. Beneath the coxcomb or his comic mask the Fool often has a power denied to others. Sir James Frazer, in his famous study of myth and ritual, describes the Festival of Fools in England and France, a ceremony which he believes to be a surviving relic of an older bid for power to insure the growth of crops. He relates this earlier ceremony to both the Festival of Fools and the Festival of the Innocents:

... a pale reflection or diminutive copy of the Festival of Fools was the Festival of the Innocents, which was celebrated on Childermas or Holy Innocent's Day, the twenty-eighth of December. The custom was widely observed both in France and England. In France, on Childermas or the eve of the festival the choristers assembled in the church and chose one of their number to be a Boy Bishop, who officiated in that character with mock solemnity. Such burlesques of ecclesiastical ritual appear to have been common on that day in monasteries and convents, where the offices performed by clergy and laity were inverted for the occasion. At the Franciscal monastery of Antibes, for example, the lay brothers, who usually worked in the kitchen and the garden, took the place of the priests on Childermas and celebrated mass in church, clad in tattered sacerdotal vestments turned inside out, holding the books upside down, wearing spectacles made of orange peel, mumbling an unintelligible jargon, and uttering frightful cries. These buffooneries were kept up certainly as late as the eighteenth century, and probably later.[68]

A dream of the Thunderbird is considered to be one of the greatest revelations and the *Heyoka Kaga* is the ceremony in which the dreamer shows his unworthiness to receive such an honor. To increase ridicule the *Heyoka* does everything contrary to the usual way. He may walk backwards; he may laugh in sorrow and weep in joy; he may wear heavy clothing in summer and go nearly naked in winter. Everything he does is usually the reverse of what is expected. This is an antithesis of behavior which is parallel to the idea of word antithesis mentioned in an earlier explanation of sacred language. Such sacred language may not be taken at its literal value, just as the *Heyoka's* actions may not be taken at their face value. In both cases, there is a mysterious power at work beneath the surface.

The *Heyoka* is obliged to declare himself one of the fraternity of Fools, for if he does not, it is believed that the Thunder Beings would strike him dead through the agency of storm and lightning. Often the Thunder Beings would "give" the dreamer a token or charm (*wotahe*), symbolic of the communion between them. The *Heyoka* would carry this at all times. Usually the dreamer received songs about his dream or the relationship between him and his totem. The following song by one of Frances Densmore's informants, Lone Man, tells of the message given him by the horsemen in the clouds, which is the form the Thunder Beings took in his dream.

[68]Sir James Frazer, *The New Golden Bough*, ed. Theodor H. Gaster (New York, 1964), p. 651.

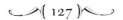

makata	The earth
etoNwaN yo	behold!
lena	All these
nitawa	yours
kte lo	will be.
makata	The earth
etoNwaN yo	behold!
lena	All these
nitawa yelo.[69]	[are] yours.

The *Heyoka Kaga* ceremony is simple though highly symbolic. The *Heyoka* indicates his intention to perform this ceremony of public humiliation by placing an offering to the Thunder Beings on top of his tipi poles. Usually the offering is tobacco, although anything of value could be used. The ceremony usually takes place in the spring, at the time of the first thunderstorms. On the appointed day, a Crier goes about the encampment announcing the ceremony. All others who have dreamed of the Thunder Beings are expected to take part in the ceremony. The Medicine Man designated to be the *ItaNcaN* (Leader) takes the *Heyoka* to a ragged tipi in the center of the camp circle. The *Heyoka* wears clothing that hangs in rags and in his loose hair he ties a bunch of sage or sweetgrass. He paints his face with black and white paint, usually in the streaked lightning design. As the *Heyoka* makes his way to the ceremonial lodge, he is followed by a jeering crowd. The older and wiser members of the tribe are not included in this group. They watch from a respectful distance and with a spirit of reverence. As the *Heyoka* tells of his dreams and sings his songs, a pot of boiling water is hung on a tripod before the ceremonial tipi. Into this pot the Medicine Man places the meat offering of the *Heyoka*, a buffalo tongue, perhaps or a dog. All those who are a part of the ceremony place their meat offerings in the pot. Lone Man explains the symbolism of the fire and the meat offering in the following way:

... the water comes from the clouds, the fire is the sun which warms the earth, the meat is from animals, which are placed

[69]Densmore, p. 161.

here for the use of the Indians, and over the pot are the clouds of steam like clouds in the sky. These are to teach the people to meditate how WakaNtaNka by these means is taking care of them.[70]

When the meat is cooked, the *Heyokas,* after rubbing their arms and hands with medicinal herbs, plunge their hands into the boiling water to get the meat. Then they give the meat to the poor, at the same time carrying on their antics like madmen. Members of the crowd accept the meat, laughing and jeering at the ragged, pathetic *Heyokas.* Only the perceptive and the wise do not laugh or scorn, for they know that the dreamers of the Thunder Beings are not burned because of the aid they receive from their totem. The *Heyokas* conclude the ceremony by singing esoteric songs, believed to be one of the sources of their dramatic power. In his songs he employs secret phrases attesting to the belief that he now belongs to the elements, and is even "worn" by them in the way that a warrior might wear a totem hawk in his hair.

he	It was
akicita ca	a guard (soldier)
wamicoNzelo	predicted for me.
tate waN	A wind
komayakelo	wears me.
waNyaNki ye	Behold it!
wakaN	Sacred
yelo.[71]	it is.

Sometimes the *Heyoka* sings that the Sioux Nation is a Thunderbird Nation (*WakiNyaN Oyate Pi Ca*), and the source of their power is the terrible bird in the sky with thunder for a voice and lightning for a flash of eyes.

Today, the *Heyoka* seems to function as both clown and scapegoat. To the less traditional Sioux he is simply a clown, much like the clown in the white man's rodeo or circus. He dresses in the familiar garb of the clown — ragged clothes,

[70]Densmore, p. 167.
[71]*Ibid.,* p. 169.

bulbous nose and facial makeup, including designs of streaked lightning. He participates in the Omaha dancing at the larger celebrations and, of course, in the celebrations following the Sun Dance. He may appear on the back of a small, decorated jackass or pony to burlesque the movements of the dancers and throw pop corn at the spectators. At the 1964 Sun Dance one *Heyoka* wore a humorous sign on his back that urged the people to vote against state jurisdiction, the major political issue of that year for the Indians. Later in the ceremony this same *Heyoka* and some of his fellows enacted a skit whose theme was the possible adverse effects of jurisdiction. A few of the older people do not find the *Heyoka* so amusing, however. They fear he may negate the good effects of the Sun Dance, or perhaps bring rain for the ceremony itself.

The *Heyoka* no longer sings his songs of the Thunder Beings publicly. Practically nothing is known, even by those who play the part of the clowns, about the songs recorded by Miss Densmore in the early part of this century. The *Heyoka* may still have songs as a result of his dream or vision, but he no longer considers these as a part of his ceremonial obligation, but rather a source of his personal power. The fact that most of the contemporary *Heyokas* are young men would seem to indicate that the older significance of the office has been lost. The writer found one older man who had served as a clown in his youth and discovered that the only song he sang at public ceremonies was one in which the single word *Heyoka* was chanted over and over again as he engaged in his comic antics.[72] Most of the *Heyokas* today are still vaguely familiar with the old ceremony but none of the writer's informants knew of its current practice.

Today, most of the older ceremonies are all but lost completely, remembered only by a few older people. This state of ceremonial neglect and dim remembrances of things past is a testimony to the Indians' degree of acculturation. Certain

[72]Joseph Thin Elk of Mission, South Dakota, in a conversation with the writer in July 1965.

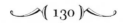

songs, customs and ceremonials are still close to the hearts of the older people and are passed on to their children and grandchildren. Often, however, even these things assume a hollow significance because the old, hunter-warrior society is gone, and most of these older songs are predicated on the existence of such a society. Ceremonials continue to be a part of Sioux life, but they tend to exist more and more for their own sakes — as a social cement or a cultural stimulus.

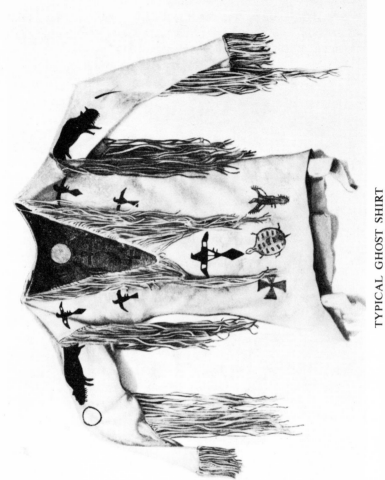

TYPICAL GHOST SHIRT

CHAPTER SIX

Songs of Cultural Change

THE SONGS OF THE Ghost Dance (*Wanaġi Wacipi*)[1] differ
dramatically from all other songs of the Sioux because they
represent a conscious, artistic attempt to throw off the chains
of what was conceived to be an intolerable present by res-
urrecting a glorious past that held in it the promise of salvation. They are the songs of a desperate vision that looks
Janus-like backward to the renewal of Mother Earth through
the intercession of the Messiah. The songs differ from other
ceremonial songs in several ways: first, within the greater
complex of the Ghost Dance ritual, they are inspired by
dreams and visions. Thus they represent a combination of
the ceremonial and individual songs — a combining which
paradoxically retains the distinctive properties of each. Sec-
ondly, the Ghost Dance songs differ from all other ceremonial songs because they alone are not accompanied by drum,
rattle or musical instrument.

The Ghost Dance complex is a classical example of a tragic
attempt at cultural renewal. It is the enacting of a drama
that has been recorded many times in blood as well as poetry.
The plaintive songs of the Ghost Dance echo the Mosaic
laments for the Promised Land, the passionate prayers of
Joan of Arc, and the nostalgic summoning of all our yester-

---

[1]The Ghost Dance was known by different names. The Comanche called
it the "Father's Dance" and the Kiowa, "Dance with Clasped Hands" or
"Dance Craziness." Among the tribes of the northern Plains the movement
was known as the Ghost Dance.

days. They echo the universal cry of the lost, and the spiritually disenfranchised as they invoke the return of the old days and the old ways. They represent the anguish and the articulation of the human kind when a fervent hope becomes a faith and a faith becomes a reality.

The ceremony of the Ghost Dance varied from tribe to tribe according to interpretive differences and imaginative resources. From other tribes of the Plains the Sioux adopted the ghost shirt, a shirt made of white cloth[2] and decorated with the symbolism of the visions of the wearer and the Ghost Dance mythology — circles, crescents, thunderbirds and other designs. The Ghost Dancers regarded these shirts as *wakaN* and impervious to the bullets of the whites. Thus, the Sioux encouraged a new element of militancy in what was originally conceived to be a peaceful doctrine of prayerful waiting.

Other tribes were critical of the Sioux for what they believed to be a perversion of the original doctrine into a warlike attitude. Even today, some of the older Sioux regard the carnage at Wounded Knee as their punishment for having adopted the Ghost Dance Religion. This feeling of guilt may be summed up in an attitude that is frequently translated into a saying: *"Wanaǵi Wacipi kiN ptecela na ocanku oeha-Nke ekta wicakagapi."*[3] The Ghost Dance is short and the road ends at burial. There are a number of good eye-witness accounts of the Ghost Dance ceremony, but the best is given by Mrs. Z. A. Parker, a teacher on the Pine Ridge Reservation, who described a dance which she observed on June 20, 1890, at the height of the Ghost Dance frenzy. The preliminary rites of fasting, painting and purification by *Inipi* had already taken place.

... the ceremonies had just begun. In the center, around the tree, were gathered their medicine-men; also those who had been

[2]Buckskin was difficult to obtain in 1890.

[3]A contemporary saying concerning the Ghost Dance, heard on the Pine Ridge Reservation. Translated by James E. Emery of Rapid City, South Dakota.

so fortunate as to have had visions and in them had seen and talked with friends who had died. A company of fifteen had started a chant and were marching abreast, others coming in behind as they marched. After marching around the circle of tents they turned to the center, where many had gathered and were seated on the ground.

I think they wore the ghost shirt or ghost dress for the first time that day. I noticed that these were all new and were worn by about seventy men and forty women. The wife of a man called Return-from-scout had seen in a vision that her friends all wore a similar robe, and on reviving from her trance she called the women together and they made a great number of the sacred garments. They were of white cotton cloth. The women's dress was cut like their ordinary dress, a loose robe with wide, flowing sleeves, painted blue in the neck, in the shape of a three-cornered handkerchief, with moon, stars, birds, etc., interspersed with real feathers, painted on the waist and sleeves. While dancing they wound their shawls about their waists, letting them fall to within 3 inches of the ground, the fringe at the bottom. In the hair, near the crown, a feather was tied. I noticed an absence of any manner of bead ornaments, and, as I knew their vanity and fondness for them, wondered why it was. Upon making inquiries I found they discarded everything they could which was made by white men.

The ghost shirt for the men was made of the same material — shirts and leggings painted in red. Some of the leggings were painted in stripes running up and down, others running around. The shirt was painted blue around the neck, and the whole garment was fantastically sprinkled with figures of birds, bows and arrows, sun, moon, and stars, and everything they saw in nature. Down the outside of the sleeve were rows of feathers tied by the quill ends and left to fly in the breeze, and also a row around the neck and up and down the outside of the leggings. I noticed that a number had stuffed birds, squirrel heads, etc., tied in their long hair. The faces of all were painted red with a black half-moon on the forehead or on one cheek.

As the crowd gathered about the tree the high priest, or master of ceremonies, began his address, giving them directions as to the chant and other matters. After he had spoken for about fifteen minutes they arose and formed a circle. As nearly as I could count, there were between three and four hundred persons. One stood directly behind another, each with his hands on his neighbor's shoulders. After walking about a few times chanting, "Father, I come," they stopped marching, but remained in the circle, and set up the most fearful, heartpiercing wails I ever heard — crying, moaning, groaning, and shrieking out their grief, and naming over their departed friends and relatives, at the same time taking up handfuls of dust at their feet, washing their hands in it, and throwing it over their heads. Finally, they raised their eyes to heaven, their hands clasped high above their heads, and stood straight and perfectly still, invoking the power of the Great Spirit to allow them to see and talk with their people who had died. This ceremony lasted about fifteen minutes, when they all sat down where they were and listened to another address, which I did not understand, but which I afterwards learned were words of encouragement and assurance of the coming messiah.

When they arose again, they enlarged the circle by facing toward the center, taking hold of hands, and moving around in the manner of school children in their play of "needle's eye." And now the most intense excitement began. They would go as fast as they could, their hands moving from side to side, their bodies swaying, their arms, with hands gripped tightly in their neighbor's, swinging back and forth with all their might. If one, more weak and frail, came near falling, he would be jerked up and into position until tired nature gave way. The ground had been worked and worn by many feet, until the fine, flour-like dust lay light and loose to the depth of two or three inches. The wind, which had increased, would sometimes take it up, enveloping the dancers and hiding them from view. In the ring were men, women, and children; the strong and the robust, the weak consumptive, and those near to death's door. They believed those who were sick would be cured by joining in the dance and losing consciousness. From the beginning they chanted, to a monotonous tune the words —

Father, I come;
Mother, I come;
Brother, I come;
Father, give us back our arrows.

All of which they would repeat over and over again until first one and then another would break from the ring and stagger away and fall down. One woman fell a few feet from me. She came toward us, her hair flying over her face, which was purple, looking as if the blood would burst through; her hands and arms moving wildly; every breath a pant and a groan; and she fell on her back, and went down like a log. I stepped up to her as she lay there motionless, but with every muscle twitching and quivering. She seemed to be perfectly unconscious. Some of the men and few of the women would run, stepping high and pawing the air in a frightful manner. Some told me afterwards that they had a sensation as if the ground were rising toward them and would strike them in the face. Others would drop where they stood. One woman fell directly into the ring, and her husband stepped out and stood over her to prevent them from trampling upon her. No one ever disturbed those who fell or took any notice of them except to keep the crowd away.

They kept up dancing until fully 100 persons were lying unconscious. Then they stopped and seated themselves in a circle, and as each one recovered from his trance he was brought to the center of the ring to relate his experience. Each told his story to the medicine-man and he shouted it to the crowd. Not one in ten claimed that he saw anything. I asked one Indian — a tall, strong fellow, straight as an arrow — what his experience was. He said he saw an eagle coming toward him. It flew round and round, drawing nearer and nearer until he put out his hand to take it, when it was gone. I asked him what he thought of it. "Big lie," he replied. I found by talking to them that not one in twenty believed it. After resting for a time they would go through the same performance, perhaps three times a day. They practiced fasting, and every morning those who joined in the dance were obliged to immerse themselves in the creek.[4]

John G. Neihardt has captured the poetry of hope and despair which characterized the Ghost Dance in his American epic, *A Cycle of the West*. It presents an interesting poetic counterpart of Mrs. Parker's description.

[4]Z. A. Parker (Mrs.), "Annual Report of the Commissioner of Indian Affairs to the Secretary of the Interior" (Washington, D.C., 1892), vol. 1, pp. 529-531.

> ... They saw the Holy Tree,
> A sapling cottonwood with branches lopped,
> Set in the center of a ring, and topped
> With withered leaves. Around it and around,
> Weaving a maze of dust and mournful sound,
> The women and the children and the men
> Joined hands and shuffled, ever and again
> Rounding a weird monotony of song,
> Winged with the wail of immemorial wrong,
> And burdened with the ancient hope at prayer.
> And now and then one turned a knowing stare
> Upon the empty dazzle of the skies,
> Muttering names, and then, as one who dies,
> Slumped to the dust and shivered and was still.
> And more and more were seized upon, until
> The ring was small of those who could not see;
> And weeping there beneath the withered tree,
> They sang and prayed.[5]

The dance step itself is different from that used in other ceremonial dances. The first phase of the dance is one of extreme simplicity, the dancers moving from right to left following the path of the sun, extending the left foot and following it with the right, the feet barely raised from the ground. It was this unusual technique that prompted the Shoshone to describe it as the "dragging step." The second phase, in which the dancers were under the influence of their visions, was characterized by a frenzied lack of restraint, each dancer following the pattern dictated by his personal vision, as described by Mrs. Parker.

James Mooney, the leading authority on the Ghost Dance, explains the visions and hallucinations as being induced by mass hypnosis. It is his contention that the shaman/priest had a knowledge, if not an understanding, of such a phenomenon.[6] Mooney was an astute, skeptical observer, thoroughly schooled in the scientific method. He devotes five

[5]John G. Neihardt, *A Cycle of the West* (Lincoln, Nebraska, 1961), pp. 48-49.

[6]Mooney, p. 187.

pages of his study to the intricacies of the hypnotic techniques employed by shamans. Mooney is undoubtedly correct in his contention that hypnosis is involved in the vision-seeking rites, yet today it seems reasonable to suggest that the hypnosis might be more appropriately regarded as self-induced. As in the *HaNblecheyapi* rites discussed earlier, fasting and intense concentration were a part of the preparation for the Ghost Dance. There was also a desperation and an atmosphere of expectation that enveloped the faithful that was almost without precedent in the rituals of a highly mystical and emotionally-centered people. Therefore, the Ghost Dance might have represented the frenzy of the exalted present.

Culturally, the Ghost Dance was the last stand of the Sioux as Indians, and they were intensely and painfully aware of this fact. The return of the dead and the restoration of what they had come to regard as an Indian Eden represented an imaginative truth so compelling that it threatened to crush the harsher realities of poverty, hunger, disease and despair. The whole complex of the Ghost Dance ritual offers one of the most dramatic examples of empirical reality being fashioned by the heart's desire into a carnival of subjectivity. The hopes and objectives of the Ghost Dance became so painfully urgent that they helped create the conditions under which they might come into existence.

It is the writer's belief that the ecstatic visions and hallucinations were self-induced by fasting, intense introspection and creative desire rather than being brought about by the hypnotic techniques of a few shaman/priests. It is also suggested that further scholarship may reveal a closer connection between the Ghost Dance and the Peyote Cult. It has sometimes been held that Peyotism arose on the Plains *when* the Ghost Dance failed and *because* it failed.[7] The effects of Peyote are very similar to the symptoms exhibited by the Ghost Dancers at the height of their expanded awareness —

[7]Vittorio Lanternari, *The Religions of the Oppressed* (New York, 1965), p. 67.

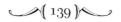

sensations of levitation, visions of brilliantly-colored images and an intense perceptual awareness of an inner reality. A close examination of Mrs. Parker's graphic, eye-witness account of the Ghost Dance and a comparison of individual behavior in this ceremony with the behavior of those under the influence of Peyote reveals a significant core of similarity.

The songs of the Ghost Dance are of great importance in any study of this millennial cult as they incorporate in their nostalgic chants much of its doctrine, tribal mythology and cherished old ways. They also reveal visionary insights into the idyllic life in the promised land. Because of their retrospective emphasis these songs paint an accurate and absorbing picture of the free, semi-nomadic life on the Plains that so fired the imaginations of those confined to dreary reservations. The songs represent not only a people's imaginative return to the past, but their hope for the future as well. The songs are highly individualized yet are also a part of the whole ritualistic performance.

As each individual dancer turned inward to confront his relatives or friends in visionary form, he made up songs about his experience with the ghosts. The passionate attachment of the Indian to relatives (particularly children) and friends and the joyful prospect of reunion with the dead inflamed the imagination and became one of the most intense anticipations in the religion of ghosts. Most Ghost Dance songs offer this expectation as a reward to the believer. Such a powerful reward is similar to the Christian promise of heaven, but it is far more specific. The names and habits of the deceased are paraded before the living in Ghost Dance songs until there seems to be a free mystical passage between the physical world and the spirit land. Most of the songs are specific accounts of encounters with people and events in the spirit world.

As has been noted in an earlier chapter, there is only one mode in primitive thought and expression — the personal. By such a method of spontaneous composition while under the influence of their visions, a single dance might produce twenty or thirty new songs.[8] Some of these songs, because of their imaginative appeal, artistry or intensity of expression were retained and became an integral part of the total Ghost Dance performance. Despite the great opportunity for variety in the ritual, there was some standardization imposed by the complex itself and the custom of retaining an opening and closing song. The Ghost Dance songs of the Sioux are all in the dialect of the Tetons because those Sioux east of the Missouri were far more sophisticated by their longer contact with the whites and were not susceptible to native appeals of such apparent naivete.

In the opening song the dancers stood still with arms reaching out to the west, the direction of the Messiah and the direction from which the new spirit world was to come. At the conclusion of this song the people of both sexes joined hands and began their dance, circling clockwise.

> Ate heye eyayo!
> Ate heye eyayo!
> Ate heye lo,
> Ate heye lo.

> NituNkaśila waNyegalake kta eyayo!
> NituNkaśila waNyegalake kta eyayo!
> Ate heye lo,
> Ate heye lo.

> Nitakuye waNyegalake kta eyayo!
> Nitakuye waNyegalake kta eyayo!
> Ate heye lo,
> Ate heye lo.[9]

> The Father says so — eyayo!
> The Father says so — eyayo!
> The Father says so,
> The Father says so.

[8]Mooney, p. 201.

You shall see your Grandfather — eyayo!
You shall see your Grandfather — eyayo!
The Father says so,
The Father says so.

You shall see your relatives — eyayo!
You shall see your relatives — eyayo!
The Father says so,
The Father says so.

Much of the doctrine and promise of the Ghost Dance is contained in this opening song. Both *Father* and *Grandfather* are terms of reverence for *WakaNtaNka* and, in the case of the Ghost Dance Religion, for the Messiah. The singers repeat each stanza four times, encouraging the presence of the Great Mystery by the use of this magical number. This version of the opening song of the Ghost Dance was tape recorded in the summer of 1964 and is practically the same as Mooney's version of 1891 and others of a later date. Of all the songs of the Ghost Dance this remains the most constant in form and content, probably because of the anxiety surrounding the ritual itself as well as the belief that this song had been "given" to the believers by the Messiah. There are other songs composed by individual dancers while in a trance, individuals who believed they had been transported into the spirit land and there had seen the Father or their own deceased friends and relatives. These songs are highly individualized and are among the most touching of all Indian songs in their pathos and simplicity.

Ina hekuwo; ina hekuwo.
Misunkala cheyaya omani ye,
Misunkala cheyaya omani ye.
Ina hekuwo; ina hekuwo.
Ate heye lo,
Ate heye lo.[10]

[9]Lloyd One Star and Singers. Recorded by Harry W. Paige in July 1964 at Parmelee, South Dakota; translated by the writer.
[10]Nancy White Horse (Mrs.). Recorded by Harry W. Paige in July 1964 at Soldier Creek, South Dakota; translated by the writer.

Mother, come home; mother come home.
My little brother goes about always crying,
My little brother goes about always crying.
Mother, come home; mother come home.
Says the Father,
Says the Father.

This song became a favorite among the Sioux and is well remembered today by the older people. The writer recalls standing with Mrs. Nancy White Horse of Mission, South Dakota, and looking across what is now Highway 18 into the small community of Soldier Creek, on the Rosebud Reservation. The old woman explained to the writer how Soldier Creek got its name: the soldiers of the U. S. Cavalry had been stationed along the creek during the Ghost Dance "trouble." As if her tale were a part of a greater drama, suddenly she began to sing the song just rendered, moving with barely perceptible steps, following the course of the sun. Tears came to her eyes as she sang, coursing down her cheeks in twin tracks. Her voice finally splintered to silence and she stood for a full five minutes gazing into the pastel brilliance of the summer day. Then she drew her dignity about her like a robe, saying that she remembered hearing that song in the "far-away times." For Mrs. White Horse, as for most of the Sioux, the Ghost Dance was dead. The songs of doctrine had mostly been forgotten, but the simple truths of the human heart — suffering and desperate desire — had remained, to be summoned up at these moments of remembering.

Another song that recalls some of the old customs is this one:

Ate michuye,
Ate michuye,
WaNhinkpe michuye,
WaNhinkpe michuye.

Ahiye, ahiye.
Wasna watiN kte,
Wasna watiN kte.
Ate heye lo,
Ate heye lo.[11]

Father, give them to me,
Father, give them to me,
Give me my arrows,
Give me my arrows.

They have come, they have come.
I shall eat pemmican,
I shall eat pemmican.
Says the Father,
Says the Father.

The composer of this song, while in the spirit land of his trance, asks the Father for some of the old-time hunting arrows with which to hunt the buffalo. "They have come, they have come." This line, and the two lines following it, indicate that the singer's plea has been granted and now he may kill the buffalo and feast on *wasna* (pemmican), that is, dried meat pounded together with cherries or berries.

The next song is perhaps the most enlightening of all the Ghost Dance songs for it best summarizes the whole hope of the movement.

Maka sitomaNiyaN ukiye,
Oyate ukiye, oyate ukiye,
WaNbli oyate waN hoshihi ye lo,
Ate heye lo; Ate heye lo.
Maka owaNchaya ukiye.

Pte kiN unkiye; pte kiN unkiye.
KaNġi oyate waN hoshi ye lo,
Ate heye lo; Ate heye lo.[12]

[11]Joseph Thin Elk. Recorded by Harry W. Paige in July 1965 at Mission, South Dakota; translated by the writer and Samuel White Horse.
[12]Mooney, p. 307.

The whole world is coming,
A nation is coming, a nation is coming,
The Eagle has brought the message to the tribe,
The Father says so; the Father says so.
Over the whole earth they are coming.
The buffalo are coming; the buffalo are coming.
The Crow has brought the message to the tribe,
The Father says so, the Father says so.

This song, perhaps the most esthetically satisfying by white standards, contains the whole message of the Ghost Dance — the coming of the renewed earth to the Indian people. The Eagle and the Crow are the sacred birds (*zitkalapi wakaN*) of the Ghost Dance, both regarded as messengers from the spirit world. An important allusion in the song is to the return of the buffalo, the most constant symbol of the old free life on the Plains. *Ate heye lo* — The Father says so — is the concluding line of most Ghost Dance songs, repeating the divine sanction and promise of the Messiah in much the same way that Christians express assent by *amen*.

The Ghost Dance among the Sioux was only a symptom: the disease was despair. A sequence of disasters without parallel in Sioux history had followed the Treaty of 1868, by which they were given all of what is now the State of South Dakota west of the Missouri River. Less than a decade after this, however, the Sioux were deprived of one third of the Great Sioux Reservation, including the sacred *Paha Sapa* or the Black Hills.[13] After the additional territorial demands of 1882, it was in 1889 that the Sioux were forced to surrender one half of their holdings, when the Great Sioux Reservation was divided into five smaller ones. In 1882 their cattle were all but wiped out by disease. In 1889 the crops failed, and this calamity was followed by racking epidemics of measles, flu and whooping cough. Also in 1889 Congress cut the beef ration on Rosebud by two million pounds, and on Pine Ridge

[13]It is interesting to note that the Sioux settlement claim for this injustice is still active in the Federal Courts.

CRAZY HORSE CANYON. ROSEBUD RESERVATION

by one million.[14] Not only were the buffalo gone, but even the deer, antelope and smaller game. Facing starvation, the once proud warriors and hunters had suddenly become "wards of the state."

Many Indian faces wore the pitted scars of smallpox, and showed the effects of the white man's liquor. The men had lost their status and dignity, and many of the women had lost their virtue to the same white men their fathers had fought against. The Sioux Nation had been reduced to a nation of beggars in less than a quarter of a century. The old, beloved free life was gone, and the future held little more than the promise of extinction. The long death had begun.

The abuses that forced the Sioux to grasp at the mystical promise of the Ghost Dance with their dying strength may be reduced to three major ones: the fear of the more traditional Indians that the old life was decaying, the failure of the government to keep its promises, and the suffering from near-starvation conditions.[15] These reasons are cited by both Indians and whites familiar with the conditions that existed at the time when the Sioux were attempting to dance back the buffalo. Commissioner Moran's report of 1891, which examines the causes of the Sioux outbreak, cites these three reasons as the basic ones which led to later violence. Dr. V. T. McGillycuddy, former agent at Pine Ridge, General Nelson A. Miles in his report to the Secretary of War, Bishop W. H. Hare, veteran Episcopal missionary among the Sioux, as well as Indians Kicking Bear, Short Bull, Big Foot, Porcupine and Red Cloud — all agreed that the outbreak of 1890 was brought on by these abuses. One of the shorter songs of the Ghost Dance gives an insight into the desperation of their plight:

Mi Ate, uNśimala ye!
Woyute kiN bluhaśni,
YatkaN miye t'a —
Oyasin henala.[16]

[14]Mooney, p. 72.
[15]Ibid., p. 69.

My Father, have pity on me!
I have nothing to eat,
I am dying of thirst —
Everything is gone.

The Ghost Dance was significant historically, culturally and artistically. Historically, its death marked the end of Indian resistance to the armed might of the government. Culturally, the Ghost Dance represented the last hope of the Sioux to resurrect the old ways. Artistically, it produced some of the finest Indian songs available.

The year 1891 is represented on the Big Missouri Winter Count by the primitive sketch of four ghosts and it is remembered as the year that marked *The End of the Indian Ghost Dance*. It might have been called *The Winter that Hope Died*, for it was an epilogue to a long and heroic struggle of the Sioux to survive as Indians. The prayer sticks that once marked the mass grave on top of the hill at Wounded Knee also marked the death of a dream and a hope. For these people who once danced to the frantic beat of their own heart's hope were no lunatic fringe. They were brave, intelligent men and women who, driven to the edge of extinction, looked toward the dying light and saw the image of the Messiah, come to deliver them. Their hopes burned again in the fires of an inner vision. In the tragedy of the Sioux there is a universality, for they simply took one of the man's oldest beliefs and gave it a native expression.

On the North American continent, as in every other part of the world, messianic movements had bloomed in the past. The desire to salvage and renovate a culture was nothing new. When the present becomes intolerable and the future holds no promise, man will turn to his past and to the mythology of his salvation. When his existence is threatened by a dominant culture, he will appeal to his gods. These things are particularly true when a primitive culture comes into conflict with a more sophisticated one. The primitive will either

[16]Lloyd One Star and Singers. Recorded by Harry W. Paige in July 1964 at Parmelee, South Dakota; translated by the writer.

resist or adapt: and either alternative may bring his complete destruction. The Seneca prophet, Handsome Lake and his Iroquois cult, *Gai' wiio*, or Good Message, founded a syncretistic movement of adaptation among Eastern Indians. Handsome Lake, like Wovoka after him, was influenced by the words of the white man's *Bible*.[17]

In 1762 the prophecies of an anonymous Delaware Indian prompted Pontiac to lead an armed expedition against the whites. In 1805 *Tenskwatawa* (Open Door), brother of Tecumseh, had a vision which formed the basis of a new cult of Indian liberation.[18] Kanakuk, the Kickapoo prophet, organized a movement based on his apocalyptic vision of the Supreme Being or Great Spirit who was at the heart of all messianic movements. Smohalla, a Nez Perce, the prophet of the "Dreamers," preached the expulsion of the whites, the return of the dead and the restoration of land to the Indian. His trances took him into the spirit world where he claimed to have seen the stars and planets, and from his dream-vision he evolved a cosmic theory of Indian salvation. It was under his influence that Nez Perce Chief Joseph led his tribe in a major uprising against the whites in 1877.[19] In 1870 the first Ghost Dance cult was founded by the prophet Wodziwob, whose high priest, Numataivo was the father of Wovoka. Thus, there is a direct link between the Ghost Dance of 1870 and the Ghost Dance that Wovoka introduced among the Paiutes.[20]

The Ghost Dance may be considered a revitalization movement, an adaptive response of a people to the onerous burdens of poverty and oppression. It represented a new impulse

[17]Lanternari, p. 102.
[18]*Ibid.*, p. 109.
[19]*Ibid.*, p. 113.
[20]Lanternari, p. 114. Actually, the roots of this movement may be traced back to earlier revitalization movements among the Indians on the Northwest Coast.

to spirituality at a time when the old gods seemed deaf to the entreaties of the people. Such revitalization movements are not isolated phenomena: they exist in Africa and in Asia today, and on those continents are closely allied to a spirit of native nationalism. These movements are both popular and revolutionary, and they often explode into dramatic prominence when the more static forms of traditional religious expression can no longer shore up the tensions to which the society has been subjected. The New Messiah frequently fits a stereotype. He is usually a native who has had close associations with the Europeans. He has absorbed some of their learning and religion. He feels a need for their gadgets, and he hates their guts. He preaches a gospel of deliverance from white oppression. He is the personification of hope to the people and whether he claims to be prophet or Messiah, the people regard him as savior until he leads them to a hollow victory or a bloody battlefield. Usually he dies a forgotten and broken man, as neglected as the soul-stirring doctrine he espoused.

For a time Wovoka, the greatest prophet of the North American Indian, traveled with a show and became a minor attraction at the Mid-winter Fair in San Francisco. In October of 1932 he died in obscurity. Periodic rumors spread among the Indians of the Plains that a Messiah had been born among them, in some obscure corner of a barren reservation. Such rumors usually come with the cold, the snow and the preparations for the Christmas season. They are imitative and usually represent the triumph of hope over bitter experience. Yet the older, more traditional Indians who see their native culture everywhere in ruins, are desperate enough to grasp at any straw. Perhaps this will be the winter, their eyes seem to say. Perhaps this will be the winter He will come to the Indian people. And so a dwindling few continue their prayerful vigil, following the bluish, winter-burning of the sun and crying:

Ate, uNśimala ye!
Father, have pity on me!

Peyotism should be seen against the background of the Ghost Dance, for the Peyote Cult was the natural successor to the Ghost Dance as the instrument of native re-adjustment to a white-dominated society. Among the Sioux, the Ghost Dance "fell to the ground" at Wounded Knee. Among other tribes, the Ghost Dance slowly crumpled into disbelief and disillusion when it became apparent that the promised Messiah had not delivered his spiritual children from their bondage. After 1890, the way of nativistic rebellion through violence was over: the Sioux were a conquered and a dying people. Any salvaging of their traditional culture had to be accomplished by a painful adaptation rather than by open rebellion. After Wounded Knee, even the most militantly native among the Sioux realized that the old path, their beloved "red road" could never be trod again, save metaphorically. The Ghost Dance had attempted to dance back the glory of a remembered past and it had failed miserably.

Some new promise of salvation was needed if the Sioux were to survive as Indians. Once again, say the believers, *WakaNtaNka* provided for his people the means of their cultural and spiritual regeneration, this time in the form of a small, turnip-shaped species of cactus variously called Peyote, Mescal,[21] the bean, the button and even the "diabolical root." Peyote *(Lophophora Williamsii)* is not native to the plains but to the Southwestern part of the United States and Mexico, most prominently along the banks of the Rio Grande River. Although it was undoubtedly used in New Mexico before its diffusion, James Mooney, the American ethnologist, reports of its ceremonial use among the Kiowa from 1891 to 1896.[22] Mooney also reports the use of Peyote in religious ceremonies among the Comanches, another tribe of the Southern Plains.

The dates of Mooney's investigations among the Kiowa are more than interesting; they are significant, for the Ghost

[21]Mescal is not the same as Peyote, although the two are often confused in the popular imagination.
[22]Slotkin, p. 34.

Dance, widely adopted by both the Kiowa and Comanche, had lost much of its force shortly before he made his study, although it survived among these people after Wounded Knee. This chronology, of course, does not establish a cause and effect relationship between the collapse of the Ghost Dance and the adoption of Peyote, but such a thesis is probable, if not scientifically demonstrable. The fact that the first ritualistic use of Peyote was reported among the Kiowa and Comanche, and that it was subsequently diffused to Indian tribes all over North America, helps define Peyotism as a Pan-Indian movement, the first such movement that has endured to the present day.[23]

It is significant that Peyotism began as, and continues to be, a native Indian religion, retaining many of the elements of the older Indian beliefs and combining these with Christian elements. The Peyote Cult or Native American Church is thus nationalistic and nativistic, the Indian version of Christianity. Psychologically as well as culturally, Peyotism combines the ways of the past with the compelling necessity of adapting to the dominant white culture. In such a light, Peyotism may be seen as a peaceful, adaptive response of the Indian to the oppressive domination by the whites.

White opposition to the consumption of Peyote began as early as 1888, when the agent at the Kiowa, Comanche and Wichita Reservation forbade its use.[24] The Bureau of Indian Affairs, the Christian missionaries, the whites near the reservations, and a large percentage of the mixed-blood population have made concerted efforts to suppress the use of Peyote. They have tried to introduce legislation in Congress to prohibit the consuming of Peyote, attempting to bring it under one of the many narcotic acts and, if this failed, to have it declared illegal under one of the food and drug acts. All such

[23]Pan-Indianism is the expression of a new identity for the American Indian and his traditional institutions. It represents an attempt to create a new ethnic group — the American Indian. Frequently, the movement manifests itself as a social and/or political movement.

[24]Slotkin, p. 52.

attempts to bring about Federal legislation have failed, although there has been some success under state laws.

White objections to the use of Peyote are usually based on three reasons: that the use of Peyote encourages nativistic practices and inhibits "cultural uniformity" and acculturation; that its ceremonial use is immoral, encouraging sexual excess, and that it is a narcotic and is thus habit-forming. Some whites also believe that the use of Peyote contributes significantly to psychotic disorders and personality maladjustments. The first objection would not seem to be a valid one in that much of the Peyote Cult doctrine is based on the Sermon on the Mount, the Ten Commandments and other Christian statements of belief. In addition, the ritual of the Native American Church venerates the Trinity and would therefore appear to be more orthodox than sects like Unitarianism. The charge that the meetings of the Native American Church are little more than sex orgies is completely unsupportable. In fact, the ethos of Puritanism is very much in evidence at these meetings and the socializing that follows. Of all the charges brought against Peyotism by its opponents, that of immorality is the most absurd.

Since the recent controversy over the hallucinatory drug, LSD, the objections to Peyote as a narcotic have increased. Opponents now link Peyote with all narcotics, attempting to suppress its use by this kind of association. There is no valid scientific evidence which supports the claim that Peyote is a narcotic, or that it has any injurious physical or psychological effects on the human constitution.[25] The Cult members feel strongly that these objections by whites and Indian non-members represent an attempt to deny religious freedom to the Indians of the Native American Church. This sentiment is frequently expressed by Indian believers who say: "The white man has taken almost everything from the Indian. Now he wants to take away Peyote, which Jesus has given him."

Every religion contains three major elements: a mythology, a code of ethics and a ritual complex. Because the Peyote

[25]Slotkin, p. 50.

HENRY CROW DOG, PEYOTE LEADER

—Harry W. Paige Photo.

Religion did not reach the Tetons until comparatively late — the early part of the twentieth century — the mythology of Peyotism is borrowed, with some variations, from the Kiowa. According to Kiowa myth, two young brothers of an unspecified tribe at an unspecified date, had gone on a war party to a distant land. When they failed to return at the expected time, their sister went off alone into the hills to mourn their passing. Made weak by fasting and sorrow, the young girl was not able to return to her people that night, and so she lay down under the open sky to sleep. Into her dream came the Peyote Spirit, informing her that her brothers still lived and if she would look the next morning in the place where her head now rested she would find the means of restoring her brothers to their people. The Peyote Spirit also gave her instructions concerning the ceremonial use of Peyote.

At the rising of the Morning Star, the girl found the cactus bud in the place indicated by the Spirit, and she took it with her to camp. There, under her direction, the holy men of the tribe set up a sacred tipi with a crescent-shaped altar on its floor. That evening the tribe held a sacred meeting with prayer and song, during which the people ate of the Peyote, multiplied many times by a miraculous power.[26] The people who ate the Peyote obtained visions and saw the young warriors, hungry and lost, wandering in enemy territory. The next morning, when the people had finished the prescribed rites, they organized a rescue party. Guided by their visions, they found the brothers, weary but safe, and brought them back to their camp. After that, the people conducted regular Peyote meetings in order to obtain visions and power for themselves and the people. The girl who had introduced Peyote to them became known as the Peyote Woman.[27] Later, when the Indians came under the influence of Christianity, the Peyote Woman became identified with Christ, especially in their parallel roles as visionaries and healers.

[26]The reader's attention is called to the parallel with the story of Christ's multiplication of the loaves and fishes in John 6: 8-15.
[27]Slotkin, pp. 22-23.

The ethical code of the Peyote Religion represents a fusion of Christian and native values and practices. It is a strict and binding code, similar in many respects to that of Puritanism. It is ironic that uninformed critics should condemn the Peyotists and their rites as immoral since the membership of this Cult is among the groups most interested in restoring a lost morality to Indian life. The ethic of the Native American Church has four main parts: brotherly love, care of the family, self-reliance and avoidance of alcohol.[28] This ethos is expressed metaphorically as the "Peyote Road," a road which leads to health, happiness and eventually, to the City of God. Brotherly love, the application of the Golden Rule, is expressed as a willingness to help others. It is also expressed by cheerfulness, truthfulness and honesty. A concern for the family, that basic unit of society, is of special importance to those who would walk the "Peyote Road."

As has already been stated, the Teton family has been subjected to a gradual process of deterioration since moving on the reservations. The father, once a proud warrior and hunter, has been reduced to a pathetic figurehead. This is especially true today since he is often unemployed and therefore cannot even pretend to his traditional role as provider. Other social evils follow hard upon the demotion of the father: adultery, broken homes, illegitimacy and neglect of children are among the conditions that threaten to destroy the fabric of Indian family life. The ethical code of the Native American Church stresses the importance of the family unit and the necessity for maintaining its solidarity. The code of self-reliance encourages the Peyotist to avoid the manifold opportunities for dependency upon paternalistic powers such as the Bureau of Indian Affairs, the welfare agencies and other organized gratuities of the white environment surrounding them. It encourages working for a living and taking a justifiable pride in one's accomplishments and the independence that accompanies them. The members of the Peyote Cult believe that self-reliance is necessary to restore the shattered

[28]*Ibid.*, p. 71.

image of the Indian male. If he can no longer be a warrior, he can be a worker. He can avoid the "hand-out" and so cancel the feeling of dependency that has haunted him for nearly a century and a half.

Perhaps the most important effect of the ethical code is to denounce the use of alcohol among believers. It is a common observation on reservations today that alcohol has killed more Indians than all the bullets of the whites. *MniwakaN*, the "mysterious water" of the whites has been, in large part, responsible for the gradual demoralization of the Indian, and it continues to be the means by which he escapes from the apparent futility of an existence in which he still finds himself in a psychological "no-man's land." "Peyote and alcohol don't mix," say the members of the Native American Church and they work militantly against the evils that the excessive use of liquor spawns. The ethical code of the Native American Church appeals to many Tetons because it stresses the older, traditional values of kinship ties (brotherly love) and the concern for the family unit. The code also presents two formidable weapons to be used against the more sophisticated attempts to reduce the Indian to emotional and economic beggary — self-reliance and resistance to alcohol. Indians who follow the "Peyote Road" also tend to exhibit the traits that reflect the overtones of such a strict code: they tend to be scrupulously honest; to abstain from profanity; to elevate the sanctity of the family, and to avoid much of the petty feuding that so frequently disrupts the harmony of reservation life.

Members of the Native American Church often seem to have a more intense awareness of their identity as Indians because their religion serves as a common bond, linking them with all other members of the North American continent. In this sense, the Peyote Cult serves to promote a spirit of Indian nationalism through its rituals, code and traditions. It is not difficult to understand how the Peyote Cult represents a peaceful, adaptive response to white domination, just as the

Ghost Dance Religion did before its objectives became perverted through violence.

The ritual of the Peyote Cult, like its code of ethics, is composed of Christian and native appeals and is, in fact, a native version of Christianity. "The white man has his *Bible* and we have Peyote," is the way that Peyote leader Richard Fool Bull expressed it to the writer.[29] The white Christian has the revelations of the scriptures, a literary account of the drama of salvation. The Indian, even in his Christianity, prefers *epiphanies*, those intense experiences of emotional upheaval that come to him through no mediator. Most of the preceding chapters of this study have attempted to demonstrate this in one context or another. From the *HaNblecheyapi* or "crying for a vision" to the Ghost Dance, there is the same intense yearning for the transcendental experience, that expanded awareness of consciousness which allows man to glimpse the reality behind the dark mirror. This is the native way — to know directly, intuitively, mystically.

The ritual of the Native American Church is designed to meet these requirements of native spiritual expression. It demands individual participation and it offers the seeker after power, visions and the ultimate possibility of direct communication with the All Powerful, the Great Mystery. There is also the possibility of entering the world of spirit, there to meet one's deceased friends and relatives, a joyful prospect that figured so prominently in the appeal of the Ghost Dance Religion. The ceremony, which Cult members refer to as a "meeting" has not changed substantially since James Mooney's description of a Kiowa rite in 1896.[30] There are, of course, intertribal as well as intratribal variations in ritual, but these are relatively minor and the complex, as a whole, remains remarkably stable.[31] The following interpretive account of a Native American Church meeting is a composite one based on the

[29]Richard Fool Bull of St. Francis, South Dakota in a conversation with the writer in July 1965.

[30]Slotkin, pp. 23-27.

[31]*Ibid.*, p. 72.

writer's observation of several such meetings held on the Rosebud Reservation.

The meetings are held in a cloth tipi in preference to a more permanent structure, thus emphasizing native tradition as a part of the complex. The entrance to the tipi faces east, as it does in most Teton ceremonials.[32] The meeting begins on Saturday evening at about eight o'clock and continues until Sunday morning. Hours before the members enter the sacred tipi, the Leader arranges the "fireplace" or altar, a raised, crescent-shaped mound of earth. With his finger he draws a straight line across the top of the mound. This line symbolizes the Peyote Road, the straight and narrow path to salvation. The Leader then places the sacramental Peyote in the center of the fireplace. The Fire Chief enters and, using cedar chips, builds a V-shaped fire while the Leader places the "tools" to be used during the ceremony on a special cloth. These sacramental objects include: extra Peyote, bits of colored cloth, an eaglebone whistle, cedar incense, a feather fan, a wooden staff, a waterdrum, drumstick, and a gourd rattle. After marching once around the tipi, the members enter and sit crosslegged on the ground floor. The Leader, who serves more as director of the ceremony than as intercessor, faces the entrance; the Drum Chief sits to the right of the Leader; the Cedar Chief sits near the fire so he may sprinkle it with incense, and the Fire Chief sits near the entrance to the tipi. The Leader opens the meeting with a prayer in the Indian language. He asks that the visions reveal God's truth to help those assembled walk the Peyote Road. Then he distributes the Peyote, which is to be chewed to a mash and eaten or brewed into a tea, depending on the amount available for the service. The Leader determines the exact number of Peyote buttons to be given to each member. He knows both the characters of the individual members and their reactions to the effects of Peyote. It is a part of his office to exert some measure of control over the behavior of the members and to pre-

[32]James Mooney feels that the Kiowa regard the Peyote button as the vegetal manifestation of the sun. This might help explain the symbolic association with the eastern cardinal point.

vent fear and panic. The Peyotist believes that a man's visions will correspond to his character. If he does evil or contemplates evil, he may see terrible powers of retribution and attempt to flee from the meeting in a panic. Each member consumes the Peyote as rapidly as possible so that he may obtain the maximum hallucinatory effects.

The ritual consists of four main parts: prayer, song, the consumption of Peyote and contemplation.[33] The prayers are not formal prayers committed to memory: they are spontaneous — conversations with God. Most of the ritual time is spent in singing. In every round of songs each member sings while holding the fan, sage and staff in his left hand and shaking the gourd rattle held in his right. While he is singing, the man beside him drums. The rhythms of the Peyote Cult music are exceptionally fast, averaging approximately one hundred and fifty beats per minute.[34] The rapid tempo is not the only distinguishing characteristic of Peyote music: the *tone* of the waterdrum produces an hypnotic effect like the *staccato* drumming of gloved fingers on a table. Many of the songs are made up largely of "meaningless" syllables. This designation, is inaccurate. For the believer, *meaning* is conveyed by what rises from the heart — the sounds that dramatize the intensity of the experience — rather than by intellectual content.

The singers are usually under the spell of their visions; often in the grip of a wild, triumphant emotion that seems to defy articulation. To the observer, the atmosphere of the Peyote meeting seems strange and unreal. It is as though the devotees were spinning a giant web of fantasy, spider-like, from the depths of their own beings. The fragrance of cedar and sage intoxicates. The waterdrum throbs like a run-away pulse. The voice of a singer rises and falls as he repeats his song in multiples of four, and, in this one particular song, he spells out the English words as the intelligible climax to his syllabic chant:

[33]Slotkin, p. 73.
[34]Henry Crow Dog, Peyote Leader of Rosebud, South Dakota.

ai na ai na a a a we na
he na ma na a a a we ne
J-E-S-U-S
O-N-L-Y
ai na ai na a a a we na
he na ma na a a a wa ne.[35]

The singing continues until midnight. When not singing, the members sit quietly in the depths of contemplation. Sometimes they stare into the fire, as though tracing a thread of smoke into some secret place where the colors sing and the sounds flow into form. One man trembles and appears to be fighting off the inner reality of an unknown terror. The Leader watches him closely for signs of panic. At midnight, the Fire Chief leaves the tipi. In a few minutes the shrill blasts of an eagle-bone whistle are heard, one blast from each of the cardinal points. The Fire Chief returns, carrying a bucket of fresh water. The Leader announces the Midnight Water Call and then offers prayers to the cardinal points. The members refresh themselves physically and spiritually as they drink from a common dipper. The Leader dips a fan of feathers into the water and sprinkles the drops on the Cult members, an action resembling the Christian baptismal rites. The Leader then delivers a sermon on Paul's Second Epistle to the Thessalonians.[36] In his broken English he reads a verse which supports the Peyote ethic:

For even when we were with you, this we commanded you, that if any would not work, neither should he eat. For we hear that there are some which walk among you disorderly, working not at all, but are busy bodies.

[35]Henry Crow Dog and Singers. Recorded by Harry W. Paige in July 1964, at Rosebud, South Dakota.

[36]The Teton peyotists are divided into two sects, Half Moon and Cross Fire. The Cross Fire sect uses the *Bible* at meetings which feature sermons; the Half Moon sect does not use the *Bible* at its meetings. The morality and ethics preached at meetings of both sects are Christian however. Other distinctions between the two sects are presented by Stephen E. Feraca in *Wakinyan*, pp. 48-49.

After the Midnight Water Call, the Leader conducts the rites of healing. The Fire Chief ushers a woman into the sacred tipi. She is suffering from severe headaches and asks to be cured. The Leader takes a Peyote button from the fireplace and consecrates it with his prayers, referring to the Peyote as *pejuta* or medicine. The woman's husband, a cult member, lights a cigarette of the hand-rolled variety. He then presents her case to the Leader, pausing at regular intervals to let the exhaled smoke drift skyward as a visible prayer. The Leader offers a Peyote button to the woman and, as she chews it, he extols the curative powers of this *wakaN* medicine, this gift from God. He presents the woman with another button wrapped in a small leather pouch: this is to be worn around the neck as an amulet, protecting her from illness and misfortune. After the conclusion of the healing rites, the water is passed around again and each one drinks. Each man then calls for as many Peyote buttons as he desires and proceeds to consume them. The singing is resumed, increasing in its hypnotic intensity as the effect of the Peyote deepens. Just before dawn the singers ask God for the benediction of His light:

> Iyoyanmpa hiyuyaye,
> Iyoyanmpa hiyuyaye,
> WakaN ta iyoyanmpa on wiconi kte — ya ya ya
> He on uwe — ye ye ya.[37]

> Send the light,
> Send the light,
> God's light that saves — ya ya ya
> So he comes — ye ye ya.

As the first clear beam of light shines from the east, the drum and rattle are passed to the Leader, who sings the Sunrise Song:

[37]William Horn Cloud. Collected and recorded by James E. Emery of Rapid City, South Dakota in July 1966 at Kyle, South Dakota; translated by William Horn Cloud.

Unpo kiN haṇhiya uwelo;
Unpo kiN haṇhiya uwelo;
Wahośiye wakaN ke haṇhiya upelo;
Unpo kiN haṇhiya hihonni yelo;
Woekicetu kiN haṇhiya uwelo;
Unpo kiN haṇhiya uwelo.[38]

Break of day is slowly coming;
Break of day is slowly coming;
Heavenly angels are slowly coming;
Break of day is slowly coming;
Resurrection is slowly coming;
Break of day is slowly coming.

In the Sunrise Song, native and Christian symbols complement each other to form an artistic whole. Perhaps one of the oldest of all man's prayers is one addressed to the unseen powers to reenact the day of creation, in which the powers of light first defeated those of darkness and chaos. For the mythopoeic mind each sunrise is nearly the same as the original event: the sun seems born again each morning. In a Christian context the Sunrise Song is a celebration of the Resurrection: Jesus, the Son of God, is risen with the new day, bearing with Him not only the Heavenly Host, but the eternal hopes of man. The song is a fine one. The formal cadence of its lines, its high seriousness of purpose and its soaring idealism are nearly Miltonic.

The Sunrise Song is chanted over and over until the sun is fully risen and the symbolic resurrection completed. The Leader then begins the closing song, which is taken up by the members and repeated in multiples of four:

Jazos, uNśimala yelo!
Nita caNku waNyanka makiye lo.[39]

Jesus, have mercy!
Lead me on your road.

[38]William Horn Cloud. Collected and recorded by James E. Emery of Rapid City, South Dakota in July 1966 at Kyle, South Dakota; translated by William Horn Cloud.

[39]Henry Crow Dog and Singers. Recorded by Harry W. Paige in July 1964 at Rosebud, South Dakota; translated by the writer.

At the conclusion of this song the Fire Chief rises and begins to remove the sacramental objects from the tipi. Once again, the water is passed around and each member drinks. A final prayer, delivered by the Leader, marks the end of the ceremony. The new day, symbolic of new hope, has risen. The Cult members appear overwhelmed by the intensity of their secret experiences: like the beholders of a dramatic revelation they seem dazed with wonder. Gradually, almost painfully, they cross the barriers of time and space into the prosaic present. Shortly after the meeting ends the families of the members appear, bearing the food and utensils for a feast that will last until noon. Even in the midst of the feasting and socializing, however, a member will lapse into an anguished silence like that of a solemn parting. He will stare abstractly into the eastern sky like a man dispossessed.

The Native American Church is not a major denomination in terms of the number of members. One Peyote Leader on the Rosebud reservation estimates that fewer than ten percent of the Christian community belongs to the Cult on that reservation.[40] The Native American Church is significant, however, as an adaptive response to white domination and as a synthesis of native and Christian elements. The movement, like the Ghost Dance before it, arose from the instinct for survival. Such survival can no longer be accomplished socially or politically; old barriers continue to break down rapidly under the weight of an advancing white culture heralded by a sophisticated technology. The human heart is the arena in which the drama for survival must now be enacted. And nothing is closer to the Indian heart than his spiritual beliefs and their ceremonial expression.

The Native American Church takes the powerful "medicine" of Christianity and gives it a native voice. Artistically, the ritual of the Peyote Cult is exciting and challenging to the observer. The songs and chants which comprise most of the ceremony are born in an imaginatively fertile climate — the inner world of vision and hallucination — and in music and

[40]Richard Fool Bull, Peyote Leader of St. Francis, South Dakota.

words reflect both the glory and the tensions of this strange realm. The artistic expression of these dramatic voyages into the unknown seemingly generates all the wonder and mystery of a revelation by Blake or a vision by Coleridge: the songs of the Peyote ritual have an immediacy, a spiritual urgency and a throbbing vitality that reveal the compelling reality of the inner experience.

Unlike the Native American Church, the *Yuwipi* Cult is essentially native rather than Christian, and represents the only widespread native cult in existence today among the Sioux. The Cult appears to be "neither vestigial nor marginal, but vital to traditional ceremonialism."[41] The word, *yuwipi* means "they wrap him up" and refers to the practice of wrapping the shaman so that he may be released by the spirits. The name also refers to the spirits themselves.[42] There is no formal membership in the *Yuwipi* Cult; membership is determined by attendance at meetings, held irregularly. Nor does membership in the *Yuwipi* Cult affect one's standing in a Christian sect.[43] While none of the Christian sects encourages such plural membership, most Christian missionaries share an attitude of resigned tolerance toward *Yuwipi*, believing that some such concessions must be made to native practices. A minority actively denounce *Yuwipi* practices as "pagan" and "idolatrous."

The purposes of the Cult are to cure illness, to find lost articles, to prophesy and, always to put on a seance-like, dramatic exhibition that serves as a diversion from the deadly routine of reservation life. Reasons for participation in the meetings are many, and often complex. One *Yuwipi* Man (*Yuwipi Wicaśa*), commenting on the motives of the Cult's followers, explained somewhat enigmatically that ". . . there are as many reasons as there are members. Each person takes

[41]Stephen E. Feraca, in a correspondence to the writer, March 19, 1967.

[42]Feraca, *Wakinyan*, p. 26.

[43]The two most prominent *Yuwipi* Men on the Rosebud Reservation are both Roman Catholics.

away from a *Yuwipi* meeting only as much as he brings to it."[44] The mythology of the *Yuwipi* Cult appears to be lost in the remote past. *Yuwipi* has undoubtedly evolved from the "dream cults" of the Indians of the Plains, cults which feature a shaman who performs magic and healing through control over his personal spirits. Parallels between *Yuwipi* practices and those of the Ojibway and Cree Shaking Tent Cults have been noted.[45] *Yuwipi* has probably developed from a diffusion of such ceremonies.

The ethical code of the *Yuwipi* Cult is not accurately defined, nor does it have to be, for this is shamanism. It consists in "always doing good," in "helping others" and other vaguely-stated generalities that could apply equally as well to native or Christian beliefs. The ritual, however, is distinctive, although, as in practically all Teton ceremonialism, it varies according to the interpretations of the individual shaman. The account presented here is a composite based on the writer's observation of *Yuwipi* meetings on the Rosebud and Pine Ridge Reservations. The *Yuwipi* ceremony is born of need — the need to cure illness; the need to find a lost article; the need for urgent counsel.

The person or persons who desire the assistance of the shaman approach him in the traditional way — by offering him a ceremonial pipe or a pouch of tobacco. While the *Yuwipi* Man smokes, the suppliant explains his request. If the shaman decides to take the case, he gives the suppliant a list of items to obtain for the meeting. The list usually includes food, a specified number of yards of colored cloth, and tobacco. Depending upon the elaborateness of the ceremony and the number of members and visitors expected, the suppliant may spend from ten to fifteen dollars on these supplies. There is an atmosphere of dramatic, exaggerated secrecy about these preparations, although even the clerks in the reservation stores know what the items are for. News of the date and time of the meeting is spread by the "moccasin grapevine."

[44] *Yuwipi* Man Frank Picket Pin of Rosebud, South Dakota.
[45] Feraca, *Wakinyan*, p. 26.

The meeting is held after dark, and after the preliminary *Inipi* or purification rites have been observed by the *Yuwipi* Man and others directly involved in the ceremony. The meeting is frequently held in a cabin on an isolated part of the reservation, a circumstance which seems calculated to add to the mystery of the proceedings. Windows and doors are covered over with blankets, small rugs or burlap bags. The room in which the meeting is to be held is barren of furniture, and the rug is rolled up against a wall. Christian statuary and pictures are conspicuously absent from the stripped room. In the center of the room is an earthen altar, laid out in a rectangle whose sides are defined by a twenty-foot string of tied tobacco packets called *caNli wapahta*. Each of these tiny cloth packets is filled with a pinch of tobacco representing prayer offerings to the spirits. The women spend the greater part of the day in the delicate work of making the *caNli wapahta* and in preparing the feast that will follow the ceremony. Positioned behind the string of offerings are five tin cans, one large one and four smaller ones. Each small can contains a pennant — red, yellow, white and black — packed in dirt. These pennants symbolize the four directions. Two other pennants — green for the earth and blue for the sky — are stuck in the large can, along with a stick several feet long to which is attached two eagle feathers. Other ceremonial objects include: a folded blanket, a pipe, a whistle, rattles, sage, a rope of sweetgrass, herbs and a single-edged razor blade.

The *Yuwipi* Man and his teenage son, who is also his assistant, enter, followed by the singers, drummers and members of the Cult. The participants and male visitors sit either on the rolled rug or crosslegged on the floor. The women and children sit opposite them on the floor. The only illumination comes from a single kerosene lamp, constantly under attack by a flurry of moths. A sharp geometry of shadows is cast on the walls and ceiling. The shaman bends over the earthen altar, arranging the string of tobacco offerings around the perimeter. At each of the cardinal points he places a sack of

Bull Durham tobacco. He then turns to those assembled, and in the Lakota language informs them of the source of his power and the vision through which this power was revealed to him. He tells the story of his vision — how, when he was a young man he saw himself carried into the sky by a great hawk (cetaN). In the other world he saw the spirits of his friends and relatives. After that experience, the hawk became the source of his power as a shaman. As he finishes his story he draws a primitive sketch of a hawk in flight, using his finger in the soft earth of the altar. The shaman's assistant passes out sprigs of sage to all, telling members and visitors alike to place the sage behind the right ear. With a dramatic flourish, he explains the reason for this: it is done so that the yuwipi will recognize the believers.

There is some concern expressed over the writer's tape recorder. After a brief conference with some of the older Indians, the shaman advises the writer to "sage" his machine, that is to drape it with sage. "It will do no good to try to record anyway," he explains. "Other waśicuN (whites) have tried it, but the spirits became angry and erased the tape."

There are grunts of assent from the membership. The shaman, his assistant, and others rub the sage on the exposed parts of their bodies. The heavy perfume of sage fills the crowded room. The shaman lights a small rope of twined sweetgrass and waves it around with all the solemnity of a bishop consecrating a new cathedral. By doing this, he purifies the people and the ceremonial objects. After filling the pipe, he presents it, stem first, to the cardinal points, the earth and sky. Two women and an older man step to the altar and accept the sacred pipe from the shaman. While each one holds the pipe with the bowl close to the body, the shaman cuts small pieces of flesh from the devotees' arms with a razor blade. The assistant rubs the bleeding wounds with sage. The shaman deposits the tiny pieces of flesh in a rattle, to be presented to the spirits for some special purpose.

Each of the votaries explains the reason for his sacrifice. The old man has a son in Vietnam and offers his flesh for the young man's safe return. The two women are sisters, sacrificing their flesh to thank the spirits for the recovery of one of their children, stricken with a serious illness. As the women finish their story, the assistant shaman extinguishes the lamp. A profound silence falls with the total darkness. A drum is struck sharply. The opening chant begins:

Oyate kiN hoye heyuya mani pe;
Oyate kiN hoye heyuya mani pe.
Wiyohpiyata: WakiNyan oyate kiN:
Oyate kiN hoye heyuya mani pe;
Oyate kiN hoye heyuya mani pe;
Oyate kiN hoye heyuya u pe;
Oyate kiN hoye heyuya u pe;
Oyate kiN hoye heyuya mani pe;
Oyate kiN hoye heyuya mani pe.

Waziyate: Hehaka oyate kiN:
Oyate kiN hoye heyuya u pe;
Oyate kiN hoye heyuya u pe;
Oyate kiN hoye heyuya u pe;
Oyate kiN hoye heyuya mani pe;
Oyate kiN hoye heyuya mani pe.

Wieyoyampata: SiNte Sapa oyate kiN
Oyate kiN hoye heyuya u pe;
Oyate kiN hoye heyuya u pe;
Oyate kiN hoye heyuya u pe;
Oyate kiN hoye heyuya u pe;
Oyate kiN hoye heyuya mani pe;
Oyate kiN hoye heyuya mani pe.

Itokataha: Tahca oyate kiN:
Oyate kiN hoye heyuya u pe;
Oyate kiN hoye heyuya u pe;
Oyate kiN hoye heyuya u pe;
Oyate kiN hoye heyuya u pe.

WaNkaNtaNhan waNbli gleska waN:
Hoye au we — e e e ya!
Hoye au we — e e e ya!
Hoye au we — e e e ya!
Hoye au we — e e e ya!
Hoye waN yuha mani ye;
Hoye waN yuha mani ye.

Maka akaNl iktomi waN:
Hoye waN yuha mani pe;
Yuha mani pe lo;
Hoye waN yuha mani pe.[46]

The tribe sends a voice as they walk;
The tribe sends a voice as they walk.
West: a Thunder Being Nation:
The tribe sends a voice as they walk;
The tribe sends a voice as they walk;
The tribe sends a voice as they come;
The tribe sends a voice as they come;
The tribe sends a voice as they walk;
The tribe sends a voice as they walk.

North: an Elk Nation:
The tribe sends a voice as they come;
The tribe sends a voice as they come;
The tribe sends a voice as they come;
The tribe sends a voice as they walk;
The tribe sends a voice as they walk.

East: a Black-Tail Nation:
    [This reference is to the Black-tailed Deer]
The tribe sends a voice as they come;
The tribe sends a voice as they come;
The tribe sends a voice as they come;
The tribe sends a voice as they come;
The tribe sends a voice as they walk;
The tribe sends a voice as they walk.

South: a Deer Nation:
The tribe sends a voice as they come;
The tribe sends a voice as they come;
The tribe sends a voice as they come;
The tribe sends a voice as they come.

Up in the air, a Spotted Eagle:
A voice is coming — e e e ya!
A voice is coming — e e e ya!
A voice is coming — e e e ya!
A voice is coming — e e e ya!
A voice you have as you walk;
A voice you have as you walk.

On earth, a Spider;
A voice you have as you walk;
You have as you walk;
A voice you have as you walk.

The voices of the singers are pitched high, almost to a discordant scream. The small, one-sided drums used in accompaniment resound like explosions. The women and children join in on the last two lines of each stanza, their voices pitched an octave higher than those of the men. The opening song contains no Christian doctrine or allusions as do the songs of the Native American Church. The allusions, the mythology and the style are all nativistic. The four cardinal points as well as earth and sky and the powers associated with the directions are invoked. There are indentifications made with the sources of power of the older, traditional culture — the Thunder Beings, the Elk, the Black-tailed Deer, the Spotted Eagle and that most mischievous of all spirits, *Iktomi* the Spider. Some of the stylistic devices of primitive poetry, discussed in Chapter Three, are also conspicuous: symbolism, allusion and repetition. The latter, especially, is carried almost to an hypnotic power.

¹⁰William Horn Cloud. Collected and recorded by James E. Emery of Rapid City, South Dakota in July 1966 at Kyle, South Dakota; translated by William Horn Cloud.

After about ten minutes of singing, the lamp is lit. The shaman announces that the invocation to the spirits has been in vain: they have failed to appear. He then proclaims dramatically that he will be bound hand and foot and will be released by the *yuwipi*.[47] The assistant and several cult members proceed to wrap the *Yuwipi* Man in a blanket and bind him securely with rope and leather thongs. They carry the wrapped shaman to the altar, and place him face down on a bed of sage. The assistant then lights the rope of sweetgrass and waves it over the blanketed form of the shaman. At a signal from the assistant, the room is plunged into darkness once more. The muffled voice of the shaman is heard invoking the spirits, calling them by name: *Iktomi* (Spider); *Pejuta Maka* (Earth Medicine); *CetaN WaNaġi* (Ghost Hawk); *Topa INyaNke* (Runs Four Times); *KiNyaN Mani* (Flying as He Walks); *CaNte Peta* (Fire Heart) and *CetaN Wicaśa* (Hawkman). The women begin to wail and moan as the room is filled with strange noises, believed to mark the appearance of the spirits. There is a loud banging, the sound of rattles and a steady whirring sound. Tiny green spurts of light seem to explode in the darkness as flying objects pass before and behind the heads of those present. The breeze from the passing objects can be felt on the face and neck. Over the confusion of sounds comes the voice of the shaman as he is heard pleading: *"TuNkaśila! TuNkaśila!"* (Grandfather! Grandfather!). The drums sound again, louder and faster than before. A frightened child cries hysterically. The flying objects come closer, spitting their greenish flame and whirring like angry fireflies. After about ten minutes of utter chaos, the noise slowly subsides and each member relates his reason for attending, followed by a request addressed to *TuNkaśila*.

The shaman punctuates the speech of the members with *hau* or *hecetu* (it is so). One woman tells of her heart ailment.

[47]Stephen E. Feraca in *Wakinyan*, p. 26, says that it is his belief that "the original *yuwipi* men specialized in being untied by small, hairy, man-like spirits." He also points out that the New York Iroquois believed in "little people" and "invoked their aid in darkened room meetings."

Another complains about the delinquent behavior of her son. A man tells of a lost wallet containing twenty dollars. When it is his turn, the writer asks about the safety of a friend serving in the armed forces.

When everyone has finished, there is another short period of noise and confusion, after which the *Yuwipi* Man, in the solemn tones of a father confessor, presents the answers that the *yuwipi* have given him. The woman is advised to throw away her medicine and place her trust in the *yuwipi*. The man who lost his wallet is told to check with the bartender at a local cafe. The *Yuwipi* Man tells the writer that his friend is safe and well. "You will get a letter from him within a week," he promises.[48] Now, the *yuwipi* are about to depart. After another noisy period of suspense, there is a flickering of light, and the shaman appears before the altar, entirely free of his bonds. Cries of astonishment and approval greet his appearance. After this dramatic demonstration of his power, he performs the rites of healing. Those to be "doctored" are ushered to the altar by the shaman's assistant. The shaman then sings one of his "doctoring" songs:

> CetaN WaNaǵi waN u ca wau yelo.
> Tuweni misumyaya wakaN śni yelo.
> "WamanyaNka po!"
> Eya uwe lo.[49]

> A Ghost Hawk and myself are come.
> Nobody is holier than I.
> "Look at me!"
> So he said as he came.

In this song the shaman goes back imaginatively to the original source of his power — the vision of his totem, the hawk. Just as the Christian feels that there are spiritual bene-

---

[48]Although the friend's letter was not forwarded from the writer's home in New York State, the postmark testified to the accuracy of the *Yuwipi* Man's prediction.

[49]Frank Picket Pin. Recorded by Harry W. Paige in July 1964 at Rosebud, South Dakota; translated by James E. Emery of Rapid City, South Dakota.

GRAVE OF CHIEF RED CLOUD. HOLY ROSARY MISSION

—Harry W. Paige Photo.

fits to be derived from re-enacting the Passion or the Last Supper, so the *Yuwipi* Man believes there is spiritual power in a dramatic and artistic rendering of his encounter with his totem. The song also illustrates the singer's belief in the power associated with going back, imaginatively or symbolically, to the original event, the source of his power. The shaman sings his "doctoring" song twelve times; in the last four renditions he is joined by the singers, and the shrill chorus of women.

Another essential part of the healing ritual is the smoking of the sacred pipe, first by the infirm and then by all—members, women, children and visitors. After several puffs on the pipe, each person repeats the ceremonial phrase, *Mitakuye oyasin!* My relatives all! An ailing man limps to the altar, complaining of stiffness in his joints. The *Yuwipi* Man takes the pipe, puffs on it and offers it, stem first, to the zenith. Then he sings his second "doctoring" song:

CanoNpa waN yuha wauwe
Mitakuye kiN iyuha zaniya onpi kte;
Ca lecamuN welo.
Tunkaśila, le miye yelo!
Miye ca ho hiyuwaki yelo,
Ca ho namahon yelo.[50]

With a pipe I come
So my relatives will all be healthy;
Thus I do this.
Grandfather, it is myself!
A voice I am sending,
So please hear my voice.

The appeal to *TuNkaśila* (Grandfather), the equivalent of the Christian God the Father, is heard frequently in these songs. After singing this song, the shaman presents some of the *caNli wapahta* to those who have been treated. He also gives bits of colored cloth, symbolic of the cardinal points, to the ill. Then the *Yuwipi* Man and his assistant dismantle

[50]Frank Picket Pin. Recorded by Harry W. Paige in August 1964 at Rosebud, South Dakota; translated by James E. Emery of Rapid City, South Dakota.

the altar, placing many of the sacred objects in a battered suitcase. A devotee enters, carrying a bucket of fresh water. As each person finishes drinking from a common dipper he repeats the ceremonial phrase, *Mitakuye oyasin*. With the act of drinking water the formal ritual ends, and the feasting begins.

The customary meat for the *Yuwipi* feast is dog — strangled and boiled with the skin on. There is also bread, soaked in canned tomatoes; potatoes; coffee and sometimes, sweet rolls or pastry. The women are busy preparing the feast before and during the ceremony. The feasting and socializing end about midnight and the people return to their homes. Arrangements are made to make the proper "donations" to the *Yuwipi* Man, pending the results of his communication with the spirits. If the suppliant's wishes are granted, he is expected to present the shaman with money or food, depending upon the importance of the favor granted by the *yuwipi*.

Both the prosperity and the reputation of the shaman depend in large measure on his success in curing or finding or predicting. Success also brings many new devotees to the *Yuwipi* Cult. Occasionally, the results are dramatic: the body of a drowning victim is located through the *yuwipi*; a woman appears cured of paralysis; two boys, lost in a blizzard, are found by following the *Yuwipi* Man's directions. Immediately, after such spectacular success, *Yuwipi* stock doubles on the reservation. Some leave the meeting spiritually refreshed. Some are apprehensive. Most are satisfied; stomachs are full. People have seen old friends and relatives. They have witnessed a drama of the old days. Boredom and despair have been dealt a blow by the *Yuwipi* Man and his performance.

As previously noted, *Yuwipi* has many variations. These depend on the knowledge, the skill, the energy, the imagination, and the success of the shaman. Sometimes, for example, there are three periods of darkness; sometimes only two. Sometimes the shaman is tied, placing the emphasis on magic and suspense; sometimes he is not tied and the ceremonial emphasis is on healing. Indeed, the writer has never seen two

Yuwipi meetings conducted in the same way. *Yuwipi*, despite its native practices and variations, deserves to be called a Cult, reflecting varying degrees of cultural change.

The *Yuwipi* Man and his followers tend to equate some of the Cult's beliefs and practices with those of Christianity. One shaman, when asked what is the power that controls the *yuwipi*, replied: "The power of God — you know, Jesus."[51] Another shaman insists that the cutting of the flesh is symbolic of Christ's blood sacrifice. The *caNli wapaḥta*, used in the ceremony, are sometimes called "rosaries".[52] *Yuwipi*, then, though in no sense a Christian cult, does have a frame of reference that is not exclusively native. Like so many other elements in the contemporary Indian culture, the *Yuwipi* Cult co-exists with Christianity, modern education, science and faith healing. Indians are a tolerant people and live easily with paradox. Indeed, the state of their contemporary culture seems built on paradox.

Evidence of cultural change may be found in ceremonies and songs that are secular as well. A good example of such a song is the one frequently referred to as the Sioux Anthem, *Ta Wapaha OlowaN*, although it is more accurate to call it the Flag Song:

> TuNkaśilayapi ta wapaha kiN oiyankeśni najin.
> Yohlate oyate kinhan wicicagin kta;
> Ca hecamuNwe.[53]

> The Grandfather's [President's] flag stands [waves] without end.
> Beneath it, the tribe continues to grow;
> So I do this.

The people sing this song at many public occasions in which the American flag is raised and/or lowered — the dedication of a new school or church, the celebration of the Fourth

[51]*Yuwipi* Man Frank Picket Pin of Rosebud, South Dakota.

[52]Feraca, *Wakinyan*, p. 32.

[53]Potato Creek Singers. Recorded by Harry W. Paige in August 1964 at Pine Ridge, South Dakota; translated by Stephen E. Feraca of Cooper City, Florida.

of July, or the funeral rites for a war veteran. The people also sing it when the distinctive, colorful flag of the Oglala Sioux tribe is raised or lowered at special functions. The Flag Song is traditional in many ways. It is brief, yet complete: it contains the essence, if not the elaboration. It is repeated often enough so that the bare three lines may take ten minutes to perform. It alludes to the United States in the older, more traditional way — as Grandfather's Land.[54] The song is sung as proudly as the National Anthem and, in its characteristically native way, expresses the same wish for our country, without the rhetoric. Hearing the song presented, one is moved by the paradox that this unpretentious, native prayer for acceptance and endurance expresses the hope of a vanquished people.

The Ghost Dance Religion, the Peyote and *Yuwipi* Cults, together with the songs that reflect their doctrines and their passions, are among the most dramatic examples of cultural change. Other curious juxtapositions, perhaps equally as vivid, could be noted in the material culture today — the horse and the automobile; the ceremonial dog feast and the picnic; the pipe and the prayer book. And there is little doubt that these changes will be more dramatic in the future. Yet there is no painless way for a culture to die. The old will always remember. The middle aged will always cast the long, backward glance, particularly when the values of the dominant culture no longer sustain them. The young will always be confused while they have a double heritage. The Teton never denies change; he knows that he cannot step on the same prairie again. But somehow knowing such things doesn't help; they still hurt.

---

[54]The President of the United States was known as *TuNkašilayapi* or "They have for a grandfather." The Congress was also known by the same name.

Afterword

THE SONGS of the Sioux have been shown to be a kind of lyric shorthand of the drama for survival — physical, psychological and spiritual. As such, they have an unmistakable universality. Modern man is not yet so far removed from his formative processes that he cannot respond to these primitive rhythms and appeals; in a sense they help him hold the mirror to a dimly-remembered self. Artistically, the songs often resemble the functional beauty, simplicity and intensity of prayer. This singing for life, though ancient, may seem to modern readers as a new use of poetry. By their directness, urgency, brevity and unadorned language something fundamental in Sioux songs speaks to readers today and frequently to people interested in the social place and the poetic means of verse.

These songs arise from the articulation of the contexts of life. Through an examination of such backgrounds as well as songs the writer has tried to help today's reader to see and feel, that is to understand something of the Indian way in song and life.

APPENDIX I

The Teton Sioux learned reading and writing from their eastern kinsmen, the Yankton and Santee, and their missionaries. Missionaries composed bilingual texts — hymnals, prayer books and translations of the *Bible* — so that the Indians might learn English, a practice encouraged by the Government through its Indian Bureau. The whites also believed that a knowledge and use of the English language would discourage the transmission of the Indian culture and facilitate Indian adjustment to that of the white man.

The Lakota language has a vocabulary of approximately 30,000 words, about the same number as in Old English. Over five hundred syllables are used to form these words, some syllables appearing as separate words, such as *wa* (snow) and *wi* (sun.)[1]

The following information, adapted from Father Buechel's *A Grammar of Lakota*, may prove helpful to the reader who might wish to follow the Lakota text.

GRAMMAR

Spelling: Because his language is not primarily a written one, the Sioux Indian is as careless in his writing as he is exact in his speaking. In the spelling of his own language, the Indian tends to imitate the English phonetic patterns of the rural dialects to which he is exposed. This confusion in spelling makes the accent difficult to standardize in writing.

[1] Eugene Buechel, S.J. *A Grammar of Lakota* (St. Louis, 1939), p. 129.

Accent: Although the rules for the accent are complicated by numerous exceptions, the following information may prove helpful. The primary accent is almost always on the first or second syllable of the word, despite its length. In almost three-quarters of the cases, the accent falls on the second syllable. A secondary accent, often difficult to detect, is used for the sake of rhythm.

Word Order: The more traditional Sioux say that the word order in English is "backwards." The Lakota word order is: subject, followed by its qualifying words; object, followed by its qualifying words and verb, with its qualifying words, which usually precede it.

Plurality: Plurality is expressed in the verb by suffixing *pi*. However, *pi* is not suffixed to the verb to express the plural of *inanimate* things. Instead, the appropriate number must be used.

Verbs: Lakota verb forms are indefinite. The time of the action is most often determined by the context, but there are two tense forms. There are no auxiliary verb forms in Lakota as in more sophisticated languages. Reduplication of the verb is common and usually expresses a repetition of the action, being or condition. The future tense, used often in Lakota, is expressed by suffixing *kte* or *kta* to the verb, e.g., *wa u* (I come); *wa u kte* (I will come). Lakota also has a progressive tense: the words *haNpi* and *yaNka* are placed after the verb to indicate a continuation of action, being or condition, e.g., *SiNte Maza lecel woglag yaNka he* (Iron Tail was talking). So time and tense of action is determined by the context or the form used.

Articles: The definite article is *kin* or sometimes *ciN*. The article follows the word modified, e.g., *wowapi waśte kiN* (the good book). The indefinite article is *waN*, an abbreviation of the numeral *waNji* (one).

Personal Pronouns: Personal pronouns may be separable or inseparable, either prefixed or inserted into the verb, e.g., separable, *Miye waśicuN* (I am a white man) or inseparable, *wamatuka* (I am tired).

Negation: Negation is expressed by placing the word *śni* after the verb form, e.g., *lowaciN* (I am hungry), *lowaciN śni* (I am not hungry).

Words for Effect: Declarative sentences frequently end in adverbial particles which mean nothing by themselves, but add rhythm and sound to a sentence. These are: *welo, yelo,* and *lo.* They are often used at the end of a brief statement, e.g., *bluha yelo* (I have it). *wicake lo* (He tells the truth). Which of these particle forms is used depends upon the letter which ends the preceding word and the sex of the speaker or writer.

APPENDIX II

Many of the songs included in this study were collected by the writer during his visits to the Pine Ridge and Rosebud Reservations in the State of South Dakota. Ceremonial songs were obtained at Sioux Indian celebrations and rites held on both reservations, which are approximately one hundred miles apart. The writer attended meetings of the Peyote Cult and the *Yuwipi* Cult, collecting and recording these ceremonial songs whenever possible. The 1964 and 1965 Oglala Sioux Sun Dances, held just east of Pine Ridge Town, were witnessed and the entire ceremonies tape recorded and photographed with the special permission of the directors. The writer also attended the Sun Dance held at Spring Creek, on the Rosebud Reservation, in June of 1965. Preparations for the ceremonies were studied and, whenever possible, tape recorded and photographed.

The traditional Lakota make every effort to conduct their ceremonials in a manner consistent with their regard for tradition and the spiritual significance attached to a particular rite. The older people, especially, tend to be quite critical of radical departure from custom, evidence of obvious concessions to tourists and general carelessness of performance. Their deep concern for tradition, as well as the prevailing belief that power is dangerous when misused, serves as a restraining influence on those who would take too many liberties with ceremonial observance. The writer compared ceremonials as performed by the contemporary Sioux with the same ceremonies as recorded by Frances Densmore and remembered by holy man, Black Elk, to determine the degree and significance of changes noted.

Some ceremonial songs were collected from a group of singers gathered together for that specific purpose — a "song meeting" as the Indians call it. Often, recording conditions at ceremonials are far from ideal (wind, noise, children playing) and it becomes necessary to resort to this technique in the interest of recording fidelity. In some cases the particular shaman is reluctant to permit the recording of songs during a ceremony. This was the case when the writer attempted to record during a *Yuwipi* meeting on the Rosebud Reservation. The *Yuwipi* Man informed the writer that the spirits to be invoked would ". . . become angry and erase the tape." However, the same shaman was perfectly willing to repeat some of his songs at the conclusion of the meeting. These recording sessions are usually held in a private home, a tent or a tipi. Singers are willing, often eager to co-operate for various reasons: some enjoy the opportunity of getting together with friends to sing; others have the performer's pride in an artistic rendition; still others are interested in having the *waśicuN* (white man) record the songs of the traditional culture so they will not be lost. It is expected that the promoters of the session, that is, those who record the songs, will provide a feast at the end of the singing. This feasting and socializing that follows the singing is an added attraction for the Indians. As the singers frequently bring their wives and families with them, the feast is usually an elaborate one.

The singers usually sit crosslegged on the floor, around a large drum. If the drum is covered with buffalo hide, special attention will be called to this fact. Some of the singers also serve as drummers, each one striking the drum on alternate beats. Sometimes the singers bring smaller drums, the kind that may be held on the lap. While performing, the singers seem oblivious to everything about them. With three fingers or a hand held against one ear to shut out some of the other voices, they lean back with heads upturned and eyes closed — the picture of an intense, inner concentration. Few of the Indian songs have any "melody" by European standards. Ethnologist and Musicologist Alice Fletcher, commenting on the esthetic gap between Indian music and the music of the West says:

Our difficulty in hearing the music of the Indian is equalled by the trouble he has with our instruments. His attention is engaged by the mechanism. He hears the thud of the hammer, "the drum inside" the piano, the twanging of the metal strings, and the abrupt, disconnected tones. Until he is able to ignore these noises he cannot recognize the most familiar tune.[1]

The converse of Miss Fletcher's observation is equally as true: the white man must learn to ignore the tune and listen to the tones of the individual singer or the isolated drum beat in much the same manner as the conductor of a musical group, who hears not only the total sound, but the sound of each separate instrument or voice as well. Most Sioux Indians sing in a high-pitched *falsetto* that to the untrained ear sounds whiney, trembling and discordant. Often, the effect created by the singers seems to resemble musical anarchy, each singer going his own way in the manner of jazz musicians. The ability to "crack" his voice is regarded by the Indians as a mark of musical proficiency, and they do this with remarkable skill. The women join in on certain repetitions that are like choruses, their voices pitched an octave above the men's.

It is possible for the informed listener to recognize some songs by qualities contained in their performance. Love songs *(Wiyoštela OlowaN)* may be recognized by the peculiar tonal quality of the singer who sings with a pronounced nasal quality that approaches a whine. Many love songs also have a discernible melody by European standards, and these can be transposed quite easily into our system of musical nota-

[1]Alice Fletcher, quoted in John Greenway, *Literature among the Primitives* (Hatboro, Pennsylvania, 1964), p. 106.

tion. Lullabies, too, have a recognizable quality of tone — a high-pitched, hypnotic sing-song that ends abruptly, almost explosively, with the single phrase, *IśtiNma ye!* Go to sleep! Omaha or Grass Dance Songs emphasize strong rhythmic patterns because they are usually performed as the accompaniments for dancing. Such songs also have a quality of masculine, dynamic progression — a quality of building to a dramatic climax. Frequently the Omaha Song will end abruptly, like an exaggerated rest in Western music, and then begin again.

Individual renditions were usually obtained in the presence of Indians knowledgeable in Lakota song, ceremony and tradition. Public criticism is still the greatest safeguard against distortion and exaggeration and it is very unlikely that a singer would render an inaccurate or incompetent version of a song before an audience of his peers. Whenever possible, translations and versions of songs were checked for accuracy and authenticity by other Indians known to be reliable and informed in native song. Some Indians have earned a reputation for integrity as well as for musical proficiency, and these were sought as informants.

ALPHABET AND PRONUNCIATION KEY

CONSONANTS

b like b in *rib*
c like ch in *chair*
g like g in *rig*
ġ like ch in German word *machen* (soft guttural)
h like h in *house*
ḫ like ch in German syllable ach (strong guttural)
j like s in *fusion*
k like k in *kill*
l like l in *lay*
m like m in *much*
n like n in *nine*
N is a nasal n, not pronounced but indicating that the preceding vowel is nasalized
p like p in *pill*
s like s in *say*
ś like sh in *shall*
t like t in *take*
w like w in *we*
y like y in *yonder*
z like z in *zero*

VOWELS

a as in *far*
e as in *they*
i as in *machine*
o as in *old*
u as in *rule*

BIBLIOGRAPHY

PRIMARY SOURCES: PRINTED

Black Elk, as told through John G. Neihardt. *Black Elk Speaks*. Lincoln, Nebraska, 1961.

Black Elk, as told through Joseph Epes Brown. *The Sacred Pipe*. Norman, Oklahoma, 1953.

Densmore, Frances. *Teton Sioux Music*, Bureau of American Ethnology, Bulletin 61. Washington, 1918.

Forbes, Jack D., ed. *The Indian in America's Past*. Englewood Cliffs, New Jersey, 1964.

Kappler, Charles J., ed. *Indian Laws and Treaties*. Washington, 1903.

McLaughlin, James. *My Friend the Indian*. New York, 1926.

Miles, Nelson A. (General). *Personal Recollections and Observations*. Chicago, 1897.

Mooney, James. *The Ghost Dance Religion and the Sioux Outbreak of 1890*. Chicago, 1965. Originally published as Part 2 of the Fourteenth Annual Report of the Bureau of Ethnology to the Secretary of the Smithsonian Institution, 1892-93, Washington, 1896.

New York Times. June 17, 1870, Sec. 1, p. 1.

Parker, Z. A. (Mrs.) *Annual Report of the Commissioner of Indian Affairs to the Secretary of the Interior*. Washington, 1892, vol. 1, 529-531.

Riggs, Stephen R. *Mary and I: Forty Years with the Sioux*. Boston, 1880.

Walker, J. R. "The Sun Dance and other Ceremonies of the Oglala Division of the Teton Dakota," Anthropological Papers of the American Museum of Natural History, 16, Pt. II, 1917.

Wissler, Clark. "Societies and Ceremonial Associations of the Oglala Division of the Teton-Dakota," Anthropological Papers of the American Museum of Natural History, II, Pt. 2, 1916.

PRIMARY SOURCES: ORAL

Arrow Side, Frank (deceased). Singer of St. Francis, South Dakota.

Black Bear, Benjamin. Singer of Parmelee, South Dakota.

Black Bear, Iva (Mrs.). Singer of Parmelee, South Dakota.

Black Elk, Benjamin. Singer of Manderson, South Dakota.

Cordry, Ernestine. Informant of Rosebud, South Dakota.

Crow Dog, Henry. Peyote Leader of Rosebud, South Dakota.

Eagle Bull, Lloyd. Sun Dance Manager of Pine Ridge, South Dakota.

Emery, James E. Song collector of Rapid City, South Dakota.

Face, John. Informant of Spring Creek, South Dakota.

Feraca, Stephen E. Informant of Cooper City, Florida.

Fire John (Chief Lame Deer). Singer of Winner, South Dakota.

Fool Bull, Richard. Peyote Leader of St. Francis, South Dakota.

Giroux, Roy. Informant of Mission, South Dakota.

Good, John (deceased). Singer, formerly of Rosebud, South Dakota.

Hawk, Margaret (Sister). Informant of Pine Ridge, South Dakota.

Herman, Jake (deceased). Informant of Pine Ridge, South Dakota.

High Pine, Matthew. Informant of Pine Ridge, South Dakota.

Horn Cloud, William. Singer of Pine Ridge, South Dakota.

Karol, Joseph (Father). Informant of St. Francis, South Dakota.

Kills-in-Sight, Noah. Singer of Spring Creek, South Dakota.

Martin, Martin (Dr.). Associate Professor of Physics, Clarkson College of Technology, Potsdam, New York.

No Heart, Andrew. Informant of Rosebud, South Daokta.

One Star, Lloyd. Singer and dance leader of Rosebud, South Dakota.

Picket Pin, Frank. *Yuwipi* Man of Rosebud, South Dakota.

Riegert, Wilbur. Informant of Wounded Knee, South Dakota.

Spotted Tail, Stephen. Singer of St. Francis, South Dakota.

Thin Elk, Joseph (deceased). Singer of Mission, South Dakota.

White Cow Killer, Ida (Mrs.). Informant and singer of St. Francis, South Dakota.

White Horse, Nancy (Mrs.). Informant and singer, of Mission, South Dakota.

White Horse, Samuel. Informant of Mission, South Dakota.

Yellow Cloud, William. Informant of Mission, South Dakota.

SECONDARY SOURCES

Andrist, Ralph K. *The Long Death.* New York, 1964.

Astrov, Margot, ed. *American Indian Prose and Poetry.* New York, 1962.

Bailey, Paul. *Wovoka, The Indian Messiah.* Los Angeles, 1957.

Birket-Smith, Kaj. *Primitive Man and His Ways.* Cleveland, 1957.

Bowra, C. M. *Primitive Song.* Cleveland, 1962.

Buechel, Eugene (S.J.). *A Grammar of Lakota.* St. Louis, 1939.

Burton, Frederick. *American Primitive Music.* New York, 1909.

Campbell, W. S. [Stanley Vestal]. *New Sources of Indian History, 1850-1891.* Norman, Oklahoma, 1934.

————. *Sitting Bull, Champion of the Sioux.* Norman, Oklahoma, 1957.

————. *Warpath.* Boston, 1934.

Collier, John. *Indians of the Americas.* New York, 1947.

Cory, David M. *Within Two Worlds.* New York, 1955.

Curtis, Natalie, ed. *The Indians' Book.* New York, 1907.

Day, A. Grove. *The Sky Clears.* Lincoln, Nebraska, 1951.

Deloria, Ella. *Dakota Texts.* New York, 1932.

————. *Speaking of Indians.* New York, 1944.

Driver, Harold E. *Indians of North America.* Chicago, 1961.

Eastman, Charles A. *From the Deep Woods to Civilization.* Boston, 1916.

————. *The Indian Today.* Garden City, New York, 1915.

Embry, Carlos B. *America's Concentration Camps.* New York, 1956.

Feraca, Stephen E. *Wakinyan: Contemporary Teton Dakota Religion*. Browning, Montana, 1963.

Frankfort, Henri, H. A. Frankfort (Mrs.), John A. Wilson and Thorkild Jacobsen. *Before Philosophy*. Baltimore, 1963.

Frazer, James. *The New Golden Bough*. ed. Theodor H. Gaster. New York, 1964.

Gilmore, Melvin R. *Prairie Smoke*. New York, 1929.

Greenway, John. *Literature Among the Primitives*. Hatboro, Pennsylvania, 1964.

Gridley, M. E. *Indian Legends of American Scenes*. Chicago, 1936.

Grinnell, George Bird. *The Fighting Cheyennes*. Norman, Oklahoma, 1958.

Harmon, George Dewey. *Sixty Years of Indian Affairs*. Chapel Hill, North Carolina, 1941.

Hassrick, Royal B. "Teton Dakota Kinship System," *American Anthropologist*, XLVI (April, 1944), 338-348.

Hoebel, E. Adamson. *The Cheyennes: Indians of the Great Plains*. New York, 1966.

Hyde, George E. *A Sioux Chronicle*. Norman, Oklahoma, 1956.

————. *Red Cloud's Folk*. Norman, Oklahoma, 1957.

La Farge, Oliver. *A Pictorial History of the American Indian*. New York, 1956.

————. *The Changing Indian*. Norman, Oklahoma, 1942.

Lanternari, Vittorio. *The Religions of the Oppressed*. New York, 1965.

Legends of the Mighty Sioux. Sioux Falls, South Dakota, 1960.

Lewis, Meriwether and William Clark. *The Journals of Lewis and Clark*. New York, 1964.

Lowie, Robert H. *Indians of the Plains*. Garden City, New York, 1963.

Malan, Vernon D. *The Dakota Indian Economy*. Brookings, South Dakota, 1963.

————. *The Dakota Indian Family*. Brookings, South Dakota, 1958.

Malan, Vernon D. and Clinton J. Jesser. *The Dakota Indian Religion*. Brookings, South Dakota, 1959.

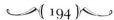

Mattes, Merrill J. "The Enigma of Wounded Knee," *Plains Anthropologist*, 5, (1960), 1-11.

McGregor, Gordon. *Warriors Without Weapons*. Chicago, 1946.

Neihardt, John G. *A Cycle of the West*. Lincoln, Nebraska, 1961.

Parkman, Francis. *The Oregon Trail*. New York, 1950.

Radin, Paul. *The World of Primitive Man*. New York, 1953.

————. *Primitive Man as Philosopher*. New York, 1957.

Sandoz, Mari. *Cheyenne Autumn*. New York, 1953.

————. *These Were the Sioux*. New York, 1961.

Sapir, Edward. *Culture, Language and Personality*. Los Angeles, 1956.

Seymour, Flora. *Indian Agents of the Old Frontier*. New York, 1941.

Slotkin, James S. *The Peyote Religion*. Glencoe, Illinois, 1956.

Smith, De Cost. *Indian Experiences*. Caldwell, Idaho, 1943.

Smith, Huston. *The Religions of Man*. New York, 1965.

Spinden, Herbert J. *Songs of the Tewa*. New York, 1933.

Standing Bear, Luther. *Land of the Spotted Eagle*. Boston, 1933.

————. *My People, the Sioux*. Boston, 1928.

Underhill, Ruth M. *Singing for Power*. Berkeley, California, 1938.

Utley, Robert M. *The Last Days of the Sioux Nation*. New Haven and London, 1963.

Wellman, Paul I. *Death on the Prairie: The Thirty Years' Struggle for the Western Plains*. New York, 1934.

Wissler, Clark. *Indian Cavalcade*. New York, 1938.

Index